The Evacuation: A Very British Revolution

To my mother who looked after me so well
during the evacuation

The Evacuation:
A Very British Revolution

Bob Holman

940.53161041

A LION BOOK

Published by
Lion Publishing plc
Sandy Lane West, Oxford, England
ISBN 0 7459 3203 7
Albatross Books Pty Ltd
PO Box 320, Sutherland, NSW 2232,
Australia
ISBN 0 7324 1246 3

First edition 1995
10 9 8 7 6 5 4 3 2 1 0

Acknowledgements
Thanks to the following copyright holders for
permission to use extracts. Every effort has
been made to trace copyright holders, and
we apologize if there are any inadvertent
omissions or errors in the acknowledgments.

Borrowed Children, St Loe Strachey, John
Murray (Publishers) Ltd, by permission of
the Publisher.

Problems of Social Policy, R. Titmuss,
HMSO. Crown Copyright is reproduced with
the permission of the Controller of HMSO.

No Cake, No Jam: A War-time Childhood,
Marian Hughes, published by William
Heinemann Ltd, by permission of Reed
Consumer Books.

Wartime Women, Dorothy Sheridan,
published by William Heinemann Ltd, by
permission of Reed Consumer Books.

Evacuees at Dartington, ed. Connolly, 1990,
© The Trustees of Dartington Hall, extracts
by permission.

Thanks to the author of 'See Thon Evacuees'
© Jenny Chaplin, for permission to quote an
extract. This article was first published in
Scottish Memories, edited by Ken Laird,
Lang Syne Publishers Ltd, 1993, and later in
Tales of a Glasgow Childhood, Jenny
Chaplin, Businesslike Publishing, 1994.

War Wives, C & E Townsend, by permission
of HarperCollins Publishers Limited

CONTENTS

FOREWORD

T hroughout the British Isles there are people who remember the war years of 1939 to 1945. Some were in the Services, some served in civilian life including services as wardens, fire fighters and members of bomb disposal squads. There were also thousands of children (and later mothers and children) who were evacuated from their homes in cities likely to be bombed to homes in the country, whether in a country town, village or hamlet, so different from their home environment. The physical and emotional disturbance was immense. The resilience of all concerned showed great courage and humour. There are, of course, many people in this country today who were born after the war who have no experience of the sorrows, trials and tribulations and wry humour of those war years. All will find this book of absorbing interest.

The late Professor Titmus, Dr Winnicott and Dr Bowlby carried out research into the effects on families and children of their wartime experiences. Their research indicated the deep social and psychological need for family life. The needs of children were foremost in the minds of legislators, administrators and indeed the population as a whole, resulting in the Children's Act 1948.

I believe that this book could well influence the way in which national policies are formulated. It should surely be read by Ministers, civil servants and legislators alike.

They will not only gain knowledge but will also enjoy the human history depicted in its pages.

BARONESS FAITHFULL

PREFACE

In September 1939 I stood in a church hall in Ipswich as an evacuee. It was in a Britain in which the Poor Law still remained on the statute book and in which there were no specialized state services for deprived children, no family allowances, no National Health Service. Twenty-three years later, in September 1962, I started work with a local authority Children's Department which was part of a well-established Welfare State. The formation of that Welfare State owed something to evacuation. The evacuation—or evacuations, for it contained three main phases—entailed the movement of up to six million people plus two million private evacuees. Most were children and young mothers. It constituted the biggest official movement of children in British history. For the evacuees it meant experiences of trauma and adventure. For the existing welfare provision it meant new pressures and ultimately new services. The intention of this book is both to re-tell those experiences and also to show how they contributed to the making of social policy. The year 1995 will witness celebrations to mark the fiftieth anniversary of the end of the Second World War. It will also mark the fiftieth anniversary of the return home of the evacuees. I should like to record my thanks to several people who gave me particular help in writing this book: to my boyhood and lifelong friend Laurie Laken; Captain Eric and Mrs Anne Buchanan; the Rev. John Whitwell; and my sister, Janet, all of whom were evacuees. Also to Lady Lucy Faithfull who, as a young welfare worker, participated in the organization of the evacuation. A special debt is owed to Maurice Lyon of Lion Publishing who encouraged me in this venture. Above all, my thanks as always go to my wife, Annette, who not only gives me emotional support and corrects my spellings, but who also finally persuaded me to give up my battered and beloved portable typewriter and to put this book on a Macintosh.

1 The First Evacuation 1939

September 1939. Britain was at war with Germany. I was nearly three and, with thousands of other children and young mothers, I had been taken to Ilford station for evacuation to Ipswich.

'Poor mite, he's got spots.'

'He's too hot.'

'Is he ill?'

'Get him some water at the next station.'

These are my earliest memories. We were crushed into a train, steam of course, in a single compartment with no corridor and so with no access to a toilet. I can recall adults and big children looming over and peering down at me. They took off my coat, unbuttoned my shirt. 'Measles,' pronounced one. Whatever it was, I never knew for I can remember no more. My sister, older than me, tells me that when we arrived at Ipswich we were taken to a hall and lined up with the other evacuees to be picked out by the women who took us to their homes.

We did not last long in Ipswich. We did not last long anywhere. Soon we were back home in Ilford for Mum and Dad wanted to keep the family together. Dad had to stay there as he was a munitions worker in Plessey's factory. Then they decided that Mum should take us to relatives in the country at Wantage. Once more on the train, then on a bus, finally a drag down a long lane to relatives whom I had never met. They lived in a small cottage with a long narrow garden which backed on to a farm. In the adjoining field pranced a ferocious bull who stuck its snorting head through the fence. Never having even seen a cow before, I was terrified and refused to go beyond the door. My fear made the relatives laugh. Probably it was the only laugh, for the cottage was too small for two families and before long we were back in Ilford in time, I believe, for Christmas.

Mum, I understand, was against further evacuation. After all, by early 1940 there was still no sign of Hitler. But Dad and his colleagues were working all hours to make aircraft parts for the fighters which were to defend Britain against the German airforce, the *Luftwaffe*, and he was sure the attack would come. So on to Bletchley, the home of one of Mum's brothers. He was away in the army but his wife and children accepted us into their council house. Mum was never happy in other people's homes. She didn't like Aunt's cooking, especially her Irish stew. One day, she decided we would eat out so, in the freezing cold with snowflakes falling, we tramped around Bletchley. We found cafes but they were all closed, possibly because of restrictions on food distribution. Going out in the evening was curtailed by the universal black-out. Once again we got the train back to Ilford. Three months, three moves, no bombs. Such was our experience of the first evacuation. But this was just the start.

The planning

My experience was typical of hundreds and thousands of others in late 1939 and early 1940. The first evacuation was under way. What prompted the Government to organize this vast movement of population? Oddly enough, its roots can be traced back to the First World War. In 1915 London was bombarded by German Zeppelins and later by planes: 1,117 civilians lost their lives. After that war, developments in both bomb and plane power intensified fears about the effects of bombing on densely-populated areas. As early as 1931, the Committee of Imperial Defence formed a sub-committee on evacuation although its plans—if any—were never published. The intervention of the German *Luftwaffe*, into the Spanish Civil War added to British concern. As the likelihood of another war with Germany grew, so questions were asked in the House of Commons as to who would be responsible for evacuating citizens away from those areas most vulnerable to aerial attacks.

As the Government vacillated, the London County Council passed its own resolution in May 1938 that it would evacuate London children in the event of war. The Government responded by appointing Sir John Anderson to chair a committee to review the matter. It soon reported that evacuation was a necessity, that it should be voluntary on behalf of the evacuees, that householders in the receiving areas could be compelled to take them in, that central government should bear the costs of the initial evacuation, and that the evacuees would be expected to contribute to their keep. Meanwhile, the London County Council, under its energetic leader, Herbert Morrison, actually started an evacuation when, following the German invasion of Czechoslovakia, it sent 4,300 nursery and physically-handicapped children to the country in September 1938. It soon brought them back.

Confusion still existed over responsibility for overseeing the evacuation. Who should decide, central or local government? At central level, which department was in charge, the Home Office, the Board of Education or the Ministry of Health? By the end of the year, the matter was put into the hands of Health under the general direction of Sir John Anderson. It soon divided Britain into three zones—evacuation, reception and neutral—and estimated that around 3,500,000 people in England and Wales and 400,000 in Scotland would need to be evacuated. It decided that priority should be given to school children (who would be transported as school units), to mothers with pre-school children, to pregnant women, and to handicapped adults. Almost immediately, some rural MPs began complaining about the expected dire effects on their constituents of being compelled to take in, as one put it, 'the dregs of London.' Some proposed large camps as a better plan. The Ministry held firm and insisted that private homes would be best for evacuee children. The Government also made clear that the responsibility for moving and receiving the evacuees rested with the local authorities—the counties, the boroughs, the district councils.

With the responsibility made clear, in 1939 the local authorities began planning. Most evacuating zones (or danger zones, as they were called) arranged for would-be evacuees to register so that some idea of numbers could be gained. Most asked for parents to put down names at their local schools. Lady Faithfull, as she now is, was then a young social worker working as a care committee organizer for the London County Council in Islington. There the children were registered in the schools but were told that any questions could be put to Miss Faithfull in her office in Pentonville Road. She tried to allay fears about the travel and the quality of the homes to which the children would go. Unfortunately, she could not tell them what they most wanted to know—their destination.

In Glasgow, 106,000 children and young mothers put down their names. The city's officials even organized rehearsals. Children assembled at the schools, waved goodbye to parents and, led by teachers, marched in lines to the railway stations—and then went back home. Manchester was particularly well organized. Audrey Jones, who recounts the Manchester evacuation, tells how the council held a series of meetings in May 1939 in order to tell parents about the plans. It was estimated that as many as 190,000 children and priority adults could be evacuated and by June the education department, which was organizing the evacuation, had listed 70 per cent of their names. One hundred and fifty buses were ordered to transport the children from 236 schools to the railway stations so that the bulk of children would be away in two days.

Meanwhile, the threat of war became more real as newspapers and radio carried stories of invasions and atrocities in Europe. Private evacuation got under way. Numbers of older and affluent citizens left the large cities to take up residence in hotels and boarding houses at coastal resorts. The even more affluent made for overseas. Southampton became crowded with elegantly-clad refugees who had decided to practise their patriotism in America. Strangely enough, if the most privileged departed early so did some of the most deprived, namely the inmates of children's homes. Herbert White, the evangelical leader of the Children's Home and Mission in Woodford, had been presented with a large holiday home in Tiptree, Essex. The children were enjoying their first holiday there in the summer of 1939 when war approached. Herbert promptly thanked God for his provision and decided that the children should stay. A wise decision, for the premises in Woodford were later hit by bombs.

The Waifs and Strays Society (now The Children's Society) had foreseen the war, held rehearsals and moved thirty of its 106 establishments before the panic. Similarly, most voluntary children's homes moved their children out of the danger zones without Government assistance. But the efficiency of their organization did not always include explaining to the children what was happening and why. Eight-year-old Marian Hughes resided in Spurgeon's Orphanage in London when she was told to get packed for evacuation. What was evacuation? They had no radio and access to no newspapers. In her autobiographical *No Cake, No Jam: A Wartime Childhood* she recalls that the only time she had heard the word was on being given medicine to 'assist the evacuation of germs in the bowels'. She helped pack the contents of the Home into tea chests, was given a gas mask, followed by a smacking when she took it to bits, and boarded a coach. Other girls told her that they were fleeing from the Germans, a threat which did not deter Marian enjoying her first ever coach ride, followed by arrival at a beautiful country house.

The evacuation order

On 31 August 1939, Hitler gave orders to his forces to invade Poland. On the same day, the British Government ordered the evacuation to start. On Friday 1 September, the evacuation machinery went into action although the official declaration of war against Germany did not come until 3 September. The Government was anticipating immediate and widespread bombing on Britain's industrial centres. Therefore the evacuation proceeded swiftly and within three days 1,473,391 persons were conveyed under the official schemes, made up of 826,959 unaccompanied school children; 536, 670 children with mothers; 12,705 expectant mothers; 7,057 blind and other handicapped persons; 103,000 teachers and helpers.

In addition, between June and September about two million other people, often adults, evacuated themselves privately. The movement was massive. None the less, the figures were not as high

as expected and not as many as registered. In Manchester, New-
castle and Liverpool about 60 per cent of schoolchildren went, in
London about 50 per cent, in Glasgow 42 per cent, and in the
Midlands only about 24 per cent.

The statistics do not convey the hustle and bustle, the excitement and laughter, the fears and the tears. Alexander Belford,
quoted in Boyd's *Evacuation in Scotland*, was a teacher in Glasgow who went with the children. They gathered at the school at
7 a.m. and then marched to the station. He described it,

*Two abreast the evacuees made their way along the streets.
Songs quickened the pace. Wishes of good luck from spectators
at windows were answered with ringing cheers. For most of the
children evacuation was something in the nature of an
adventure ... The only worried people were the mothers and
fathers.*

Most evacuees were conveyed by train. The stations were cram-
med full with children, with labels attached, carrying sandwiches
and the inevitable gas masks in cardboard boxes. Forty-four
million gas masks were issued during the war and were never
used. Some parents at the stations were beset by anxieties. They
had seen newspaper photos of the effects of bombing in Spain and
China and believed this could be the last time they saw their
children. Ben Wicks, himself an evacuee, in *No Time to Wave
Goodbye* tells of one tragic family whose father had just died and
whose funeral was the day of the evacuation. The mother was so
worried about the bombs that she insisted that her children went
on the morning evacuation even though they had to miss the
funeral. Even so, at the last moment some mothers changed their
minds and dragged their children away.

Eric Buchanan, later to be a Salvation Army captain in Glasgow—where we became close friends—remembers it much more
clearly, for he was ten at the time. His father, an ex-regular soldier
from Glasgow, and his mother lived in a block of flats, the Lewis
Trust Building in West Kensington, London. Eric had a twin sister,
a baby brother, an older sister who joined the land army, and an

older brother who went into the airforce as a pilot where he was killed. Eric told me:

We got fitted with gas masks. My wee brother got a Mickey Mouse one. Great excitement when we heard about evacuation. We had to give our names in at school and then mum got a list of the things we had to take. For the first time ever I had a school cap and a raincoat. On the day, I went to the school with my twin sister and mum. Funnily enough, nobody would tell us where we were going. We got on a bus with the teachers to Olympia railway station. Masses and masses of kids and mums. All with gas masks in brown boxes and string. We had lots to eat on the train. They even gave us a bar of chocolate. We made it to Bath and Bristol and then to Chew Magna where we made our way to the village hall.

Given the numbers involved, it was not surprising that some confusion and delays occurred on the railways. The worst feature concerned the lack of water and toilets on journeys which took several hours. One non-corridor train from West Ham was bound for Somerset but the needs of the children were so great that, when the train made an unscheduled stop at Wantage in Berkshire, the children poured out to make for the toilets. In other trains, boys pee'd out of the windows. What the girls did is not recorded. Food and drink soon ran out, children began complaining, teachers' tempers became frayed. Mr Belford recalls that after a while:

. . .paper comics, ceasing to appeal, were thrown aside. Grimy and tired, the children became fractious. Babies began to fret and mothers to worry . . . At last the train slowed down. All crowded to the windows to see what the place was like. Fields, fields everywhere; a few cottages, then streets and shops. 'Miss, please miss, are there any sweetie shops?' 'Aw I dinny see any picture houses.' 'My, it's just a wee toon.'

Mr Belford was fortunate compared with one of his colleagues who wrote:

*The journey from Glasgow was the most depressing, deplorable
and disgusting journey I have ever had the misfortune to make.
The train took twelve-and-a-half hours to reach Aberdeen.
Half-hours and hours were spent in railway sidings until the
line was clear ... The evacuees were famished when they
arrived, having had no food for a matter of twelve hours. (Most
of their food had been eaten before leaving Glasgow.) The
babies-in-arms kept howling for milk which was unobtainable
at any station. Mothers began to grow hysterical ... Many
children became train-sick. There was a lack of water on the
train. On arrival at midnight, the evacuees, teachers and
helpers were so exhausted that the term 'refugees' applied to
them by some of the householders seemed more appropriate
than offensive.*

Lucy Faithfull was employed to get the children on to the trains.
But twice the volunteers who were due to travel with the children
did not turn up. She explained,

*I had to go with them. Once to Marlborough. We had a number
of pregnant mothers on the train and I got worried when one
said she thought the baby was coming. I had not the slightest
idea what to do. 'Don't worry, ducks,' she said, 'I've three
already.' She had it an hour after we arrived.*

*The other time I went to Oxford. The children were billeted
but there was nowhere for me. Eventually a woman took me in
at Cowley. I said to her, ' I'm terribly sorry but I haven't got a
night gown.' There was a look of extraordinary battling in her
face then finally she brought me a most beautiful night gown
and said, 'This is my burial night gown and I'll let you have
it.' I felt awful for I could see what a great sacrifice it was for
her.*

Not all evacuees went by train. Some climbed on to coaches
and double-decker buses. Children from Dagenham boarded
boats and sailed down the Thames to Felixstowe in Suffolk. In
Glasgow, some journeyed down the Clyde as recalled by one

evacuee, Jenny Chaplin, in 'See Thon Evacuees' in the magazine *Scottish Memories*:

> *We were taken from Glasgow's Govan by bus to a ferry terminal somewhere down the Clyde coast, where in a rare old state of excitement, we boarded a boat for the next stage of our journey. Most of our school-mates had never before been out of Glasgow in their young lives, far less travelled on a boat. In that respect at least, my wee bree, Telfie, and I were luckier than our companions. We were already experienced travellers, having been 'doon the watter' the previous summer on a never-to-be-forgotten holiday to Rothesay. Of course, even we realised that there was a vast difference between a holiday sail on a Clyde steamer when the ship had been brightly painted, dressed overall with flags and bunting which waved in time to the ship's band; and a war-time boat painted battleship grey and with not so much as a German band or a destination board in sight.*
>
> *Nobody thought to tell us where we were going—it was war-time after all, and it had already been instilled into us that 'careless talk costs lives', so we knew better than to ask any questions. So as we sailed across the Firth of Clyde, we had no idea as to what would be our eventual fate or even where we might lay our weary heads that bedtime.*
>
> *As is often the way in such situations, rumour was rife. And no doubt aided by the vivid imaginations of some of the big girls and 'Qualy boys', we younger weans were soon in a panic—totally convinced that we were being kidnapped by 'thae durty Germans' and never again would we see Mammy, Daddy nor Glasgow again.*
>
> *I remember it vividly . . . all the port-holes had been boarded over, we could see nothing beyond the saloon into which we were herded and the grey-painted ship was grim and unwelcoming. And as if all that were not enough, add a rough crossing with scores of tearful children being sea-sick, as well as already home-sick for the familiar and now far-away streets of Govan; scared out of their wits at the thought of the*

*rumoured goose-stepping Germans now supposedly marauding
the decks above our heads . . . take all these things together and
you get a clear picture of our situation.*

*Apart from our own teachers, our minders included a
motley crew of young students, clerks and Sunday school-
teachers who had been pressed into service in this emergency.
They were having their own not inconsiderable problems in
trying to cope efficiently with a mixed load of fractious and
terrified evacuees.*

Probably these horror stories were not typical although they did
happen. The fact is that over a four-day period some 4,000 trains
plus an unknown number of coaches and boats were mobilized and
succeeded in getting all the children to their destination. The
exercise was a tribute to the civil servants, local government
officials, the teachers, the volunteers who travelled with the
children, the Women's Voluntary Services who helped out at the
stations, and the railway staff. And to the mothers and children
who set out not knowing where they were going or when they
would be back.

The reception

Once the whistles were blown, the waving subsided and the trains
on their way, the organizers in the evacuation zones could con-
gratulate themselves on having done their bit. But theirs was the
easier bit. The problems were to be even more serious at the
reception end.

In the reception zones, the county clerks and town clerks had
appointed chief reception officers who, in their turn, appointed
assistant reception officers for each station (or pier) and billeting
officers for each district. But they laboured under certain handi-
caps. The Government had given a bland assurance that it would
underwrite any costs for the evacuees' boarding but it was not clear
whether this covered associated costs such as, for instance, any fees
for medical treatment. Clarification did not come until after the
children arrived. The local authorities, ever reluctant to spend
money, had not prepared extra maternity units, hospital places and

reception centres. In some instances, provision had not even been made for extra school places. Further, they appeared to have little information on how many evacuees were coming, what kind and when. Professor Richard Titmuss, the official historian of the home front, in *Problems of Social Policy* had to conclude, 'Many reports testify to the general confusion and unpreparedness which characterized the reception of the mothers and children.'

On the appointed day, many at the reception end were left waiting for hours. Some, expecting babies and mothers, received schoolchildren. School parties were split up and arrived at differing and various destinations where they were not due. The boat children from Dagenham came in far larger numbers than anticipated and some pupils had to be put into temporary accommodation in schools without bedding or blankets. On some stations there was such disarray that some mothers eventually took their children to the opposite platform and caught a train home. By contrast, on a few stations complete peace reigned, as at the one where the reception officer waited with an army of volunteers for 3,000 evacuees and not one came. In a diary kept for the organization Mass Observation, and quoted in *Wartime Women*, Muriel Green recorded the arrival of evacuees to a small Norfolk village on 3 September. She wrote, 'Evacuated mothers and children arrive in village from Shoreditch and Hoxton. Wrong trainload arrive—only children expected. Organisers have great difficulty in getting people to take them in.'

Once they did make it to the stations, the evacuees were herded to local halls where, usually, they were given some refreshments. Then started the selection process, the part of the exercise which became seared into the memories of evacuees. The prospective foster mothers, as they became called, had taken it for granted that they would select their boarders. As one put it, recorded in *War Wives*:

> My husband was on the committee for placing the children with local people. He had asked if I would like girls or boys, dark or fair, blue eyes or brown. I (smilingly) replied, 'Two girls—fair hair and blue eyes, please.'

18

And she got what she wanted. Ben Wicks in *No Time to Say Goodbye* writes:

As one of those who suffered the humiliation of waiting to be picked, I know that it is something I will never ever forget. With many of the children who were left unchosen, it seemed there was nothing to do but gather them up and begin a walk from door to door. The strange sad lines were a common sight as the billeting officers or teachers tried their best to find someone willing to take them in, if just for the night.

When I interviewed Eric Buchanan who generally spoke positively about the evacuation, he was also upset by the manner of selection:

The people to foster us were waiting in the village hall. That was hairy, not knowing who we would get. My twin sister was separated and I went on my own to a couple just outside the village. At night the wind blew the curtain about making a strange noise and I was scared.

Eric did not last long in that foster home.

The selection process seemed designed to emphasize the power of the foster parents and the powerlessness of the evacuees. The latter had had no choice in their destination and, once there, no say with whom they would lodge. My sister tells me it happened to us but I cannot recall it—perhaps I blocked out a painful memory. As Titmuss records in *Problems of Social Policy*:

The war-time guests of the country were further aggrieved when, in many areas, they were walked or paraded around while house-holders took their pick. Scenes reminiscent of a cross between an early Roman slave market and Selfridge's bargain basement ensued.

Jenny Chaplin and her brother had an even more humiliating experience, as she recalls:

If we had thought the voyage was bad, even worse awaited us once we were safely ashore. No, it was not the Germans of our imagination who turned out to be the enemy—but rather the well-meaning officious ladies and gentlemen, the 'high heid yins' otherwise designated as our Billeting Officers. Their first remit was to herd us all into a draughty church hall, there to await the next step in processing us from City weans to bona-fide Clyde coast evacuees.

Young as I was, it soon became clear to me that the high heid brain who had master-minded the operation had obviously equated material poverty and a working-class district in Glasgow with filth, vermin and neglect. So, following this line of thinking, it was deemed essential that before we could be allocated to our host homes where we could be 'welcome', we must first be de-loused.

On all sides I could see terrified small boys having their heads shaved and being left with an obscene tuft of hair sticking up at the front. As for the girls, they did fare a little better in that they were being given pudding-basin haircuts and the compensation of a can-can fringe.

I felt sick as I watched this operation. Not only that, I felt dirty, degraded and finally, very angry. Was it for this that Mammy had spent Daddy's hard earned money on Derbac soap and the special steel comb, with which she industriously searched our hair for nits and other such live-stock every Friday night?

Fortunately, Telfie and I were at the end of the queue and as the shearers approached, wild thoughts went racing through my brain. Finally, when escape seemed impossible, I decided on a spot of positive action. Taking a firmer grip on my brother's hand, I bent down to his level, then whispered a few words in his ear. As I recall, it was a somewhat garbled message all about horrible giants, 'thae durty Germans' and their shears with which they would cut us both up into little pieces and throw us to the sharks in the river!

Whatever my hastily whispered words meant to Telfie, I'll never know, but they must have helped him to conjure

*up some pretty weird mental picture in his tiny mind.
Anyway, the end result was that we both yelled, screamed,
scratched and kicked to such good effect that eventually we
were left to our own devices ... and still in proud possession
of a full blown head of hair apiece. Telfie's golden waves
and curls still bounced across his now tear-begrutten face;
while my crop of beribboned sausage-ringlets must have
stood out as an affront to the unnecessary carnage scattered
around us.*

The public hair examination and cutting was not general. But in
every hall there would be a child left to last or a small group who
did not get chosen at all. Lucy Faithfull always felt pain on their
behalf and said, 'I used to go up to that child and say, "You're so
important that you are the last one to be chosen." What the child
made of that I don't know.'

Probably, the stories of confusion and pain remain stencilled
most deeply in human memory. Matters did proceed more
smoothly in some reception zones. In Cambridge, the city's education officer had taken on the role of chief billeting officer and
had made careful preparations. Officers were put in charge of
each ward in the city and instructed to survey them to see what
accommodation was available. As befits a university city, public
lectures were delivered on the subjects of the health, nutrition
and treatment of children. Transport was arranged to convey the
evacuees from the station to the assembly halls. On 1 September,
the trains started arriving on time at 11.30 a.m. and the machinery moved into gear.

Generally, the arrangements worked smoothly. Hiccups did
occur. The organizers had overlooked that some evacuees were
coming by coaches and forgot to book lodgings for the drivers.
On the first evening, a few young children had to be placed temporarily in an institution for the aged and infirm. But even that
worked well for they were made very welcome by the kindly
matron and residents. The organizers even coped with fourteen
different languages for the evacuees included refugees from
abroad. The city had been told to expect 8,000 children over a

three-day period. In the eventuality, less than half that number came, a reduction which eased problems considerably.

In country districts, the reception and distribution activities had to be separated into two distinct parts. The evacuees were met at the station and then divided into groups to be driven to village halls, scattered all over the counties, for the selection of foster homes. One of the earliest books on the evacuation, *Borrowed Children*, was written in June 1940 by Mrs St Loe Strachey who drew together the experiences of herself and other well-to-do country ladies. One wrote:

We waited in the village hall from two till five. Tea and lemonade was prepared: also a churn of milk, cocoa and biscuits. While we waited, the Billeting Officer and reception committee went through the list of those who had volunteered to receive unaccompanied children ...

Members of the committee, and many others, put in last minute pleas for 'one quiet little girl of about nine' or boldly volunteered to take a boy, provided he was scrupulously clean and small enough to cuddle. But when, at last, someone ran in crying, 'They've come and they're all big boys' —I think we were most of us jogged at once out of our selfishness, and out of the imaginative paralysis induced by prolonged crisis. I know that my own heart beat stronger, and my eyes filled with tears, as they marched in—nearly eighty of them. They were dirty and unkempt, and many of them ragged: but they held their heads high, and carried their rucksacks and bulging pillow-cases with a swagger.

I settled down to work with one of the masters; and immediately those eighty children became for me mere names to be attached to names of hostesses. I hardly saw the children themselves, who were ranged on benches drinking lemonade. But I grasped that there were a few girls after all, and some small boys—tagged on to their elder brothers in this Senior Boys' Section of a big Dockland Council School.

It took us an hour and a half to dispose of all the children, and by that time some of the smaller ones were crying. One eight-year-old's nerves had snapped under the long day's strain; and he had hurled his belongings—followed by a shrill stream of oaths—out of the car that was taking him to his new home. Brought back in disgrace, he was now snuffling quietly in a corner. Beside him stood his big brother, one of the best and most intelligent boys in the school—his serious, open face sweating with shock and family shame.

There were two others whom I noticed, because whenever they pushed forward to announce that they had found a home and were going off to it, the presiding master ominously ordered them to wait. But for my part, I saw nothing beyond my lists.

My own home, owing to a delay in returning the form, was not down to receive any children. But my husband and I invited two of the masters to come back with us, and to bring such of the boys as could not at the moment be placed. And in due course we carried home our 'spoils'—two exhausted masters, and seven very tired little boys. Of these seven, two were brothers, whom the masters dared not let out of their care, owing to their bad record—the two who had so often been turned back; and one was the eight-year-old whose blasphemies had shaken the respectable village street.

The kindness and patience of this reception area was evidenced elsewhere. A young London school teacher, evacuated with her class from Walthamstow, was another one to keep a diary for Mass Observation. What she recorded at this time is quoted in *Wartime Women*:

May I say how exceedingly kind were these people. Just a little example of this was shown when a lady, outside whose house we had been dumped, furnished all the kiddies with bread and jam! It was at 9.45 p.m. when we managed to get the last child of our batch settled for the night and he, poor chappie, was in a state of collapse. During those memorable five hours the weather clerk had decided that a little rain would perhaps afford a little light

relief. Needless to say we had no time to consider whether it
dampened our meetings or not.

I was fortunate in securing a billet that night with people
who, having passed us in their car when we were leaving the
distributing centre, had relieved the kiddies of their rucksacks
and ration-bags (these consisted of
1 tin Ideal Milk, 1 tin bully beef, 1 packet biscuits, 1 bar of
chocolate). These kind people followed us around in their car
and relieved the kiddies of their belongings whilst waiting to
be fixed up with a billet. It seemed incredible to me that no
arrangements had been made for teachers and we had to
depend on people's kindness of heart to supply us with
accommodation for the night. Ah well, our quest was ended at
10 p.m. and when I arrived at my billet I set to and wrote off
new addresses to the Walthamstow parents. The day had been
a memorable one indeed.

So somehow most evacuees were found somewhere to stay for
the night. But this was just the start. It could hardly be expected
that the rushed arrangements would lead to perfect harmony—not
even in Cambridge where it was recorded in *The Cambridge
Evacuation Survey* of 1941:

By September 3rd the Evacuation Department of the
Guildhall and the Ward Billeting Officers were being
inundated with complaints from all sides, and from then on
these places have continued to function as clearing centres
for difficulties.

One whole street returned all their children after one night
and refused to take any more. Then there was the matter of the
undergraduates' lodgings. The Evacuation Department had
esti-mated that there would be a great reduction in student
numbers and so persuaded traditional student landladies to
take evacuees.

Soon after, hundreds of extra students arrived as other colleges
evacuated from the large cities to Cambridge. The landladies

preferred students and so over five hundred evacuees were turfed
out and had to be found new billets.

It was the same in other places. Foster mothers protested
that they had been promised girls but got boys; babies and got
adolescents; children on their own and got their mothers as
well. In Scotland, some foster mothers were affronted to
receive children of the wrong church denomination. The
billeting officers patiently, if wearily, promised to sort matters
out. Simultaneously, they and their colleagues were trying to
draw nearer together children from the same schools who had
been scattered all over the country. The teacher from
Walthamstow, quoted in *Wartime Women*, was in despair
when, after three months, she still had not a meeting place for
her children. She penned in sarcastic mood,

> *It was not until we came into contact with the rural councils
> that we congratulated ourselves on the magnificent
> efficiency and administration of Walthamstow's Education
> Committee.*

It should be remembered that the officials were also trying to
arrange maternity units, obtain extra medical staff, persuade the
Government to pay bills, and a hundred other tasks. They deserve
thanks for tackling a task for which they had no experience or
training. And so do the foster parents. There was to be friction
between foster parents and evacuees but, in those early days, many
opened their doors with willingness and gladness. The Mrs St Loe
Stracheys with their maids and insistence on being called hostesses
not foster parents played their part, often from a mixture of
compassion and patriotism, as is recorded in *Borrowed Children*.
One tells how she had been promised 'a helper, no boys and six
girls of about nine.' She received four girls, four boys and no help.
She kept them. Another volunteer had driven the evacuees to
remote country farms and, when she returned home, found that
seventeen small girls and two teachers were still without lodgings.
But, she recorded in the tones of middle-class, country Britain at
its best:

*The day was warm, my daughters active, my cook and
housemaid full of kindness. There were camp mattresses, we
had prepared an immense stew, we had a bread-cutting
machine, and (happy days) plenty of butter.*

She took them all in.

The return

All the excitement was in the reception zones. What was happening
in the danger zones? Not much danger for no bombs were dropped
and the period became known as the phoney war. It is instructive to
read *The Ilford Recorder*, the weekly paper in my home borough in
these months. Three items dominated its pages. First, the black-
out. With the *Luftwaffe* expected any moment, September 1939
revealed officials almost paranoid that not a chink of light should
be exposed at night. The manager of a pub was prosecuted for not
properly darkening his windows—he had covered them in in-
effective brown paper, not black curtains. It was reported that a
policeman touring the streets on his bike had spotted the brown
paper and promptly marched into the pub and ordered all the lights
to be turned out. The manager complied and his customers
continued drinking. When the policeman continued to tell him
that he would be prosecuted, the manager demanded to know his
number and, when the constable refused to give it, struck a match
so as to see. The policeman, horrified at the exposure of yet more
light, promptly blew it out and took the offender to the police
station. At least this story has a funny side. Not so amusing was a
serious accident to a 71-year-old woman who fell down her stairs in
the black-out. Then there were motor accidents at night. Road
accidents increased by over 100 per cent in the black-out.

Second, the borough council bewailed its financial state. The
paper agreed and, in an editorial, explained that many conscripts
and adult evacuees had left without paying their rates, that the
council had had to fork out for the construction of air raid shelters
and was paying weekly wages totalling £4,000 to its ARP workers,
and that the council had borne many of the costs of the evacuation.

Third, there were cheerful stories about the evacuated children.

A billeting officer was quoted as saying that the Ilford children were enjoying a 'healthy life'. Ilford County High School had been evacuated to Suffolk and the paper published a long letter from a senior pupil saying how wonderful the billeting officers and foster parents were and that the whole expedition was 'a glorious holiday'.

By October, however, the evacuation cheerfulness began to fade. Parents complained about the difficulties of visiting remote Suffolk villages. One of the paper's reporters attended a mothers' discussion about the evacuation and wrote how they had scoffed at the broadcast words of the politician, Miss Horsbrugh, who said that parents with children at public schools would not dream of unsettling them by making visits and nor should the parents of evacuees. The mothers pointed out that the rich chose the public schools but they had not chosen their children's foster homes and they wanted to visit to see what they were like. Soon after, parents, including those of pupils at Ilford County High, were writing in to say that their children felt 'unwanted' in Suffolk and suggesting they be brought home.

In a November edition of *The Ilford Recorder*, next to a notice announcing National Rat Week and encouraging all Ilfordians to kill as many rats as possible, there was an article which focussed on the adult evacuees, the teachers and young mothers. Prominence was given to their grumble that their landladies were charging them extras and so making it impossible for them both to live as an evacuee and to maintain a home in Ilford. Soon after, the Women's Co-operative Guild petitioned the Director of Education to bring back the children and to re-open schools in Ilford. He hinted that he would probably do so, for by this time many evacuees were returning under their own steam.

The Ilford experience was representative of what was happening all over the country. By January 1940, only 55 per cent of the unaccompanied children and 12 per cent of mothers with children were still evacuated. In all, 61 per cent had returned home. In Scotland, the return was even more rapid, so that by January only 11 per cent of all the evacuated children were still there. And the drift home continued throughout the spring.

What accounts for the return? One obvious reason is that mothers with young children often felt very uncomfortable in another person's home. The foster parents or landladies were expected to provide them with lodgings only—unless they came to an extra financial agreement for meals. Usually, the mothers were expected to provide their own food and to share the kitchen. Such sharing was not easy and led to disagreements. Mothers then tried to buy meals outside but often cafes could not be found in small villages. The local authorities were slow to establish social centres where mothers with small children could meet. It followed that often the only place the women could find refreshment and company was the pub, but attendance there opened the mothers to the criticisms that they were flirting with local men and taking their children into, or leaving them outside, public houses. Not surprisingly, it was the mothers who led the exodus back to the cities.

Another reason was that unaccompanied children simply missed their parents, homes and neighbourhoods. Evacuee children in Cambridge were asked to write essays about the evacuation. Some enjoyed it but nearly all said that they missed their families and many mentioned that they missed their friends, their pets, football in the street, the cinema, and the chip shop. Clearly some wrote to their parents asking to go home. Sometimes parents would visit and, seeing the unhappiness of their children, took them back on the spot.

The strongest reason, however, was that the bombs had not fallen. The evacuation was a response to the expectation certainly of immediate bombing and probably of invasion. Air raid warnings and rushing to shelters had been practised. The black-out had been enforced. Machine-gun posts, barbed wire and concrete tank blockades had rapidly been installed. Posters and radio warnings told citizens to beware of spies. The atmosphere in August and September 1939 was of attack at any moment. In *No Time to Wave Goodbye*, Ben Wicks tells of one evacuee who was met by a vicar and transported in his car: the boy had never been in a car before and mistook the diagram of gears on the gear stick for a swastika. He reported the sign to the police who took it seriously enough to interrogate the bewildered vicar at the police station as a suspected spy. But the vicar wasn't a Nazi. The planes did not come in their hundreds. Shots were never fired from the pill boxes. The evacuees began to question the very basis of the evacuation. What was the point of sharing another woman's kitchen or of being separated from the kids? As the psychiatrist Donald Winnicott explained in one of his war-time broadcasts, mothers not only love their children, they also need them. Without the reality of bombs there was no point in being apart. They went home.

Was the first evacuation a waste of time? In the report *Problems of Social Policy* Richard Titmuss thought not, for he argued that it served as a rehearsal for the time when the bombs did drop. And drop they did.

2 The Blitz and the Trickle

As 1940 proceeded so the phoniness went out of the war. Rationing was introduced and I got used to the routine of Mum looking for food ration books, finding them in one of the drawers of the sideboard, and then joining the queues with a reluctant me in tow. I can recall the butcher marking off the coupons with a thick blue pencil.

In the spring, Hitler's forces invaded Denmark and Norway. A British landing in Norway ended in failure. Winston Churchill, ironically with more enthusiasm from Labour MPs than Tory ones, replaced Chamberlain as Prime Minister and on 13 May delivered his famous speech:

> *I have nothing to offer but blood, toil, tears and sweat. You ask, What is our policy? I will say: It is to wage war, by sea, land and air, with all our might and with all the strength that God can give us ... You ask, what is our aim? I can answer in one word. Victory—victory at all costs, victory in spite of all terror; victory, however long and hard the road may be.*

Churchill's only rival had been Lord Halifax who might have negotiated for peace. Not so Churchill. The British people now knew for certain that the war was for real until defeat or victory. And just then it looked more like defeat. Even while Britain was changing its leader, Hitler's forces were sweeping through Holland and Belgium and advancing on to France. In response, British and other Allied troops counter-attacked into Europe where they were out-flanked and overwhelmed by their opponents. There followed in June the famous maritime retreat from Dunkirk. Over 68,000 lost their lives while 474 planes and six destroyers were lost. Meanwhile, much of France was occupied and the German forces were just across the Channel.

Invasion now seemed certain. In the summer, the Home Guard was formed and quickly enrolled one million members. The Home Guard has now been affectionately and comically displayed on TV as *Dad's Army*, a load of elderly, inept yet lovable buffoons. The programme also conveys their courage and rightly so. Churchill's command to them was to go down fighting with the injunction, 'You can always take one with you.' Many resolved and expected to do just that, even if their weapon was a broomstick. Meanwhile, parents watching newsreels of German planes machine-gunning Dutch civilians could feel relieved if they had insisted on leaving their children in evacuation. But many had not and the subject came to the fore again. The Government hastened to send children from London's East End overseas to Canada and the USA. Some adult citizens also joined in and, as A.J.P. Taylor records in *English History 1914–45*:

> *... 1,000 women and children from the richer classes went privately at their own expense. Members of the Government and university professors sent their families on this unseemly scramble.*

The crossings were also extended to other parts of the country and working-class parents were able to nominate their children for the sea voyages. On 1 August the liner *Volendam*, carrying 320 evacuee children, was torpedoed by a U-boat in the Atlantic. Amazingly, the ship did not sink and eventually tugs were able to tow her back to Britain. Seventy-four of the children were Scottish and were brought back to Greenock. Two weeks later, they joined other children on *The City of Benares* sailing from Liverpool. Sadly, it too was attacked. The ship went down and seventy-seven children drowned. Forty-six children spent eight days on a lifeboat in cold and stormy conditions before being rescued. Thereafter the crossings ceased.

One family which refused to leave Britain even when offered the chance was the Royal Family. King George VI practised with his revolver in the grounds of Buckingham Palace, where he was prepared to die fighting. His intention reveals the common expectation in Britain that invasion was nigh. Certainly Hitler intended just that but, before doing so, his plan was to use air power to smash Britain's defences. In August, he ordered the *Luftwaffe* to destroy the RAF's fighter bases in the south-east of England. There followed the famous Battle of Britain. I remember standing in the street with my dad watching some of the dogfights as British Spitfires and Hurricanes took on German Messerschmitts and Junkers in clear blue skies criss-crossed with vapour trails. Then Dad would rush indoors to listen on the radio to the scores as the BBC announced how many planes of each side had been shot down.

It always seemed as though the RAF were winning although it is now known that the BBC exaggerated the extent of German losses. Indeed, given the shortage of British pilots, the result was in the balance when Hitler suddenly changed tactics to concentrate on bombing London. Christians attributed his decision to the intervention of God and even A.J.P. Taylor called it 'a miraculous event.'

The Germans had undertaken spasmodic bombing raids during the summer of 1940 but the Blitz started in earnest on 7 September 1940 when 625 bombs containing one hundred tons of explosive descended upon London. The docks and factories in the East End took the brunt of the attack with 430 civilians killed and 1,600 seriously injured. The next evening the bombers returned, with the raids spreading out to take in West London and the suburbs. They droned over for seventy-six consecutive nights, save for 2 November when the weather was too bad.

Initially, the bombers had it easy. The RAF fighters were not equipped for night fighting while the anti-aircraft guns, although noisy, made few hits. The only resource for most people was to take shelter. Many fled to their Anderson shelters which were, by now, a familiar sight in back gardens. They consisted of curved walls of corrugated steel sunk three feet into the ground. They were then covered in earth in which grass and weeds soon sprouted, and some keen gardeners even cultivated flowers and vegetables. The Andersons were effective against blast but not against a direct hit. Many citizens did not possess gardens so the local authorities had constructed brick and concrete shelters for public use. Being above ground, these shelters were not regarded as safe and many Londoners preferred to make for the tubes, the underground stations. Of course, many were not near tube stations and some people who lacked an Anderson, particularly the elderly, would shelter in their cellar or under a table.

One night as we returned from our shelter in the garden, I looked at a London skyline which was almost completely red. It must have been 9 December when 1,600 fires raged. As a small child I was fascinated by the almost-beauty of it all. A terrible beauty, for the fires spelt death for many. This curious mixture of the colour and terror which made up air raids has been brilliantly described by Angus Calder in *The People's War:*

> *First, there was the alert, a wail rising and falling for two minutes, 'warbling' as the official handbook somewhat inexactly put it. There was not one siren but a series, as the note was taken up by borough after borough. Then, there was the heavy, uneven throb of the bombers. 'Where are you? Where are you?' Graham Greene imagined them saying. Then there were many noises. The howling of dogs; the sound of a high explosive bomb falling, like a tearing sheet; the clatter of little incendiaries on roofs and pavements; the dull thud of walls collapsing; the burglar alarms which destruction had set ringing; the crackle of flames, a relishing, licking noise, and the bells of the fire engines. Each individual A.A. gun, to the increasingly sensitive ears of Londoners, had its own voice. One set near John Strachey's warden's post in Chelsea was called 'the tennis racket' because it made 'a staccato, and yet plangent, wang, wang; wang, wang.' The shells shrieked and their splinters pattered on the pavements. A bomb falling half a*

mile away gave you ten seconds' warning by its swish and rush through the air, but the one 'with your number on it', the one which killed you or buried you alive, was heard only when it was almost upon you, because the sound waves caught up with themselves.

Outside, if bravado or duty sent the citizen outside, there was a world of beauty; Charlotte Haldane has said that for her, the 'aesthetic pleasure' which the fires provoked 'banished all sense of fear'. 'The sky over London,' as Evelyn Waugh saw it, 'was glorious, ochre and madder, as though a dozen tropic suns were simultaneously setting round the horizon ... Everywhere the shells sparkled like Christmas baubles.' Searchlights crossed and recrossed in stiff and awkward arcs, plunging thousands of feet into the sky, each terminating in a 'mist area' which reminded Harold Nicolson of 'a swab of cotton wool'. The raiders, to begin with, would drop parachute flares, magnificent fireworks which drifted slowly down in a constellation, illuminating earth and sky with an amber or greenish light and casting exotic shadows over grubby and familiar townscapes. Suddenly, a street would be carpeted with brilliant incendiaries, hissing and sparkling with a whitish green glare. A high explosive bomb, by comparison, was disappointing; its upward streaks of yellow or red were as crude as a little boy's painting of Guy Fawkes' Night (a fixture which few citizens found it hard to forego on November 5th). Once, in October, a bomb struck a gasholder in the south. Five thousand cubic feet of gas burnt in a couple of seconds, and 'an enormous uprush of white light, like a gigantic mushroom with a huge black cap' suddenly towered over London.

Calder does not mention parachute bombs perhaps because the Government tried to disclaim their existence and did not allow newspapers to name them until 1944. Parachute bombs were simply land mines attached to parachutes. They were particularly deadly in that they descended with no noise and might lie hidden until disturbed when they then gave an enormous and forceful explosion.

Ilford experienced thirty parachute bombs between September 1940 and May 1941. The first fell on 21 September and was spotted by an air raid warden, a Mr L. Miles. He rushed towards it shouting to people to get clear. The mine exploded on landing, leaving Mr Miles severely injured. He continued to direct operations to combat the flames but died soon afterwards. He was posthumously awarded the Gold Cross. Soon after another mine fell into a back garden without exploding. Most people were already in their shelters and the wardens had to get them out and move them out of the area. Naval bomb disposal experts came but it was not until the afternoon of the following day that residents were allowed back into their homes.

Two parachute bombs fell in our road although I did not realize it at the time. Once reporting restrictions were lifted, *The Ilford Recorder* revealed that:

> one of the most horrifying experiences of the whole Blitz in Ilford was experienced. Civil Defence men worked desperately to reach a man who was trapped under the wreckage, which was alight.
>
> This man, conscious all the time, lay helpless and watched the flames creeping nearer and nearer to him. He was got out but was badly burned.

The craters made by these two bombs were forty feet deep.

The worst incident, however, was when a parachute mine landed directly onto the public house, the Prince of Wales, in Chigwell Row. *The Ilford Recorder* stated that:

> It was a Saturday night, and the house was full. More than 60 people lost their lives and included among them were several members of the Clayhall Cricket Club, whose rendezvous it was. Pieces of clothing were flung high in the air, and dangled from the tree-tops. There was nothing left of the public house.

It seems that the parachute mine had drifted in from a distance, had not been spotted and hence no air raid siren could be sounded.

Even today, fifty years later, I cannot hear an air raid siren without a sense of fear and chill. Then my mother would drag me out of bed and lead my sister and myself down the garden path to the shelter. We would be joined by the lady next door, whose husband was in the army, and her mother. One night, as we all assembled together, our neighbour screamed at a dead mouse on the ground. My inner mind, young though it was, laughed at a woman who screamed at a mouse but not at the bombs which were screaming all around us. My dad, a very practical man, had not thought much of Anderson shelters and so had built his own. It was dug completely underground, with concreted sides, and an air vent to the surface. He had also built in bunk beds so we were warm and comfortable. It was difficult to sleep both because of the noise of planes and bombs and also because of the fear that one had your number on it. But I tried to read an old book—one of the few we had—which was the history of King Alfred in pictures. I read by candlelight and sometimes must have dropped off to sleep, for often, when I awoke, I was back in the bedroom.

Sometimes we risked not going to the shelter. Perhaps we were too slow in getting out of bed. One night, the planes were low and noisy, the explosions all around. Mum tried to drag us down but Dad stopped her. We stood hand in hand on the landing with Dad saying, 'If we go, we go together!' The windows were blown in by shrapnel as a bomb fell nearby. A lull. We dashed for the shelter.

Perhaps Dad was slow in getting up because he was worn out. As well as working long hours operating a machine in the factory, he was also in the ARP, an air raid warden. In the evening, and often through the night, he and his colleagues patrolled the streets on the look-out for incendiary bombs which the *Luftwaffe* now dropped as well as explosives. Sometimes Dad would show me the shell of one. They were surprisingly small, like a metal bottle. But on impact they burst into flames and it was these which sparked the massive fires. The wardens would try to pinpoint where they dropped, inform the fire brigade and bravely, if foolhardily, try to smother them with blankets. The wardens were also there after the all-clear sirens joining other civil defence staff to dig out the wounded and dead from the rubble. Dad would sometimes come in exhausted and dirty with his grey features showing the harrowing experiences which he must have endured but about which he would not speak in front of the children. But it had its lighter moments and I did hear him telling his mates how, on entering one bombed house, he was called over by a woman who promptly took down her knickers and asked him to pick the glass out of her backside. His mates roared with laughter—Mum was not so amused.

The wardens had a small building, made of breeze blocks, just over the road from us. Here they met to plan the evening duties and to report back. Here too Dad took up playing darts, a sport he was to enjoy for the rest of his life. The wardens often popped into our home. I can envisage them now: one was a tally clerk in the docks; there was the local cobbler; and Curly who, of course, was as bald as a coot. Their comradeship was to continue after the war when they always came round on Saturday evenings to play cards and when they formed a darts team. Their friendships made in the dangers of the Blitz lasted until their deaths.

The bombing raids went on so long that we developed a kind of routine. In the morning, Mum would check that the gas, electricity and water was still on. We were mindful of not wasting these commodities and it inspired in me a habit, which I still have difficulty in abandoning, of washing in two inches of water. After a cup of tea and a slice of bread and marge, Dad left for the factory. Then we made for the shops with Mum, who always managed to get something with her ration books and gift of the gab.

On the way, we would see housewives sweeping glass and other debris into piles for council workmen to collect later in the day. More frightening was the sight of the houses which, as my dad would say, had 'copped it'. Rescuers might still be digging, workmen pulling down dangerous walls, public utility staff trying to locate the gas leaks, and all amidst a still rising cloud of dust and smoke. Then, even at 10 a.m., there were long queues at the bus-stops as people tried to make their way to work.

Most firms had not moved out of London. In addition, half a million munitions workers were still there. Their staff regarded it as a war-time duty to get to their jobs. The factory where my dad laboured was just a few minutes away but others depended upon trains whose tracks had been bombed, upon trolley buses whose overhead wires had come down, and upon buses always vulnerable to blast. So many of the London red buses were damaged that buses of all colours were brought in from other cities. The queues might be a hundred yards long with the workers not knowing what time they would get back home that night or, indeed, if there would be a home still standing.

At our home, too young to go to school, I stayed with Mum and watched as she skilfully used the rationed food to make an evening meal for Dad. I listened for his footsteps at the back door. After the meal, at which we all had to sit at the table, he would sink into his armchair with his cup of char and the newspaper. I often liked to stand behind him, combing his hair, until he shooed me away and made his way to the ARP post. Mum then got some blankets out ready for the nightly trip to the shelter.

Sometimes, I would see schoolboys searching amongst the rubble for shrapnel and I would try to join them before Mum's hand on my collar dragged me back. Play in the midst of death. Marian Hughes, living in London, illustrates this in her autobiography *No Cake, No Jam: A War-time Childhood*. She wrote,

We were now very conscious of the war, which had taken on a new significance. There had been a lull in the frequency of the raids, but now suddenly sirens seemed to sound almost every night. We hadn't ever been to the shelters; Mummy vowed she never would. Our windows, like everyone's, had strips of paper pasted cross-wise all over them, and at dusk we would have to draw black-out curtains. When Anthony and I pulled them aside to watch the searchlights, we heard the sharp retort, 'Put that light out!' It was a phrase we were to hear many times. We sometimes heard bombs falling with a tremendous wallop, but mostly they were in the distance, but Anthony and I were not at all afraid—for now.

The war became part of our adventure playground. The two of us would wander about with a morbid curiosity after an air raid, hoping to see somebody dead. One day we were watching

the demolition of an unsafe building. A crane swung over us,
lifting an iron bedstead, and the body of a young soldier rolled
off and fell at our feet. His face, covered in fine dust, looked
like that of a well-fed child asleep.

We ran away and never spoke of it.

Things got worse, and eventually we did go to the shelters.
In one air raid, Dorothy and Anthony had just run off (for
some reason I stayed behind), when a huge blast blew out our
windows. Part of the ceiling came down on Mummy. For a
moment she just sat there, with blood slowly oozing from her
head. I watched in horror, not daring to move. Suddenly she
stood up, clenching her fists, and delivering fearsome curses to
Hitler! Her voice screamed above my fright; her eyes dilated
and her energy was awesome. I found her more terrifying than
the bomb.

The church and the bombs

Amidst all the death and destruction, it was astonishing that so
many people stayed in London. The Government wanted non-
essential workers and families to leave. Apart from a concern for
their safety, it was also worried about dangers to health in the
unhygenic and crowded shelters. During 1940, officials toured
shelters and knocked on doors to persuade more people to accept
evacuation but with limited success. Some families had already
experienced evacuation and could not face the separation again.
Further, efforts were being made to make life in London more
bearable.

The efforts initially came less from the public authorities, who
were overwhelmed coping with the effects of bombing, and more
from voluntary bodies. The Salvation Army, the Red Cross, and
the Women's Voluntary Service opened rest centres, community
centres and respite places for those rendered homeless by the
bombing, where food, blankets, beds and advice, were immediately available. The large shelters in which many people gathered
in the evening began to take on a life of their own with community
singing and even soloists. One enormous shelter in Stepney was
crowded beyond capacity with up to 10,000 people gathered in it.

They elected a shelter committee with a well-known local character, Mickey Davis, as leader. Mickey was an optician, a hunchback, three feet, three inches tall. He proved an inspired choice and soon Marks & Spencers installed a canteen which not only served the evening callers but also distributed milk to children in the day. The shelter had become a community centre. In this and other large shelters, film shows, music and dancing took place. On quieter evenings, some people would visit other shelters on a kind of shelter crawl.

Probably church ministers were the most active in organising collective action during the Blitz. Father Wilson of Haggerston opened his church hall, although it was not an official shelter, and it was soon crowded, with the participants so enjoying the food, card games and other entertainment that they refused to leave during the bombings. The Anglican Pacifist Fellowship founded its Hungerford Club underneath the arches where shelter and food was provided for thousands of those then called 'vagrants'. The church centres provided shelter and friendship while the presence of ministers was a comfort to some whose daily rounds brought them constantly into touch with death and suffering.

The best-known clergyman at the parish level was Father John Groser. A High Anglican priest who had spent much of his life in East London, Groser was a radical who was often at logger-heads with both spiritual and secular authorities. As president of the Tenants Defence League in Stepney he had joined forces with the communist, Tubby Rosen, in the 1938 rent strike against private landlords. He was just as forthright during the war. When bombed-out parishioners had no food, no fuel and no power—for the local shop had been destroyed—officials were slow to respond. Groser promptly took the law into his own hands, smashed open a local food depot and then lit a bonfire outside his church on which to cook meals. Later, he broke open an empty block of flats in order to house those made homeless by the bombs. Simultaneously, Groser was opening his church halls and ministering to individuals who were bereaved, wounded and dying.

Other priests and ministers of all denominations opened their churches and counselled the needy during the Blitz. What made

Groser different in 1940–41, was his ability to see what was happening, to put an interpretation on events, to insist that good could come out of evil. Groser was already established as a preacher, lecturer and writer and he began to take issue with those who claimed that the terrible war with all its suffering was evidence of the non-existence of God or of the powerlessness of God. Instead, in his book *Politics and Persons* he argued that the Blitz was drawing social classes together, and was showing the authorities just how valuable and heroic ordinary people were. Out of this, he foresaw, would come social reform, a better life for all and hence the creation of something more like the society which God wanted on earth. He agreed that they had all prayed to avoid war but, he added:

> at last it engulfed us, and miraculously set us free. It is one of the mysteries of history: a mystery which I believe is only explicable in terms of a living God active in history.

'Coventrated'

It was not just London that suffered the Blitz. Some historians consider that if Hitler had continued to focus on the capital then he would have brought it to its knees. Yet again, Hitler changed his tactics at a crucial time and decided to bomb other parts of Britain with the result that some pressure was taken off London.

In October 1940, the *Luftwaffe* made raids on the Midlands. On 25 October, Birmingham was attacked and 170 people lost their lives. Then it was Coventry's turn. By now Germany had settled on a raiding method which entailed that the first planes in a raid, guided by radar beams, served as pathfinders by dropping incendiaries on the target area. Then came the main force of bombers. In an attack lasting ten hours, 400 planes dropped 30,000 incendiaries and 500 tons of explosives. The city was gutted. The medieval centre, the beautiful cathedral, the industrial and residential zones were all heavily bombed. Over a third of the city's houses were rendered uninhabitable while a third of the city centre was flattened. So fierce were the fires that 200 firemen were injured and twenty-six died in putting them out. In all, 554 people were killed and 865 seriously wounded. The word 'Coventrated' passed into military jargon to mean that a town had been razed to the ground.

The effect of bombing on medium-sized and compact towns like Coventry was even more devastating than on London. After just one night, nearly everyone knew somebody who had been killed, injured or made homeless. Mass Observation reports, which were suppressed at the time, recorded that in Coventry 'There were more open signs of hysteria, terror, neurosis, observed in one evening than during the whole of the past two months.' With up to 500 retail shops destroyed and the massive loss of ration books as well as buses, trains and roads being put out of action, the bomb victims, for the first time, faced hunger. As many as 100,000 loaves were rushed in from nearby cities and the WVS was soon there. Fortunately the Germans did not repeat the attack. Coventry's citizens adapted and, amazingly, a week after the attack, five-sixths of local employees were back at work. At the Morris Motor Engines Works, where the roof had been shattered, they continued to produce tank engines under the open skies even when snow was falling. The burnt cross, still standing in the cathedral, stood as a symbol of Coventry's resistance.

Bristol had suffered small raids but its main turn came on 24 November. Birmingham again. Then Southampton, Merseyside, Sheffield, Portsmouth, Leicester. Attacks did not stop on London. On 29 December came what was to be known as 'the second fire of London' when the City burned but St Paul's Cathedral survived. The New Year of 1941 witnessed attacks on Portsmouth, Cardiff, Manchester and Swansea. Then came the terrible raids on Glasgow and Clydebank on 13–14 February. Glasgow suffered badly but the smaller shipbuilding burgh of Clydebank even more so. Its population tended to live in crowded tenements and hence damage to people and buildings was intense. All but seven of its 12,000 dwellings suffered damage. The human cost was enormous—35,000 of its 47,000 population were made homeless and many sought safety on the outlying hills. Amongst the 500 killed were children who had returned from the evacuation. Yet soon the workers were back at work at John Brown's Shipyards.

Raids occurred all over Britain. On 20–21 March, Plymouth's town centre was blasted and then the city suffered again five times in April. As many as 30,000 people were made homeless and hundreds trekked to the frozen moors to escape. Scores of other towns were hit before, on 10 May, London endured its worst night. On that night, more than two thousand fires raged from Hammersmith in the west to Ilford in the east. A third of the streets became impassable and 150,000 families were left without gas, water and electricity. The next morning the sun was blotted out by palls of thick smoke. It was as though it was in mourning for the 1,436 persons who had died. On the evening of 11 May, fire crews were still fighting the fires from the night before. Another raid of that ferocity might have finished London. Yet once again, the final blow was not delivered.

It was not the end of the bombing. Smaller raids continued including the 'tip and run' raids by fighter bombers on coastal areas. Later, in the spring of 1942 came the Baedeker (or 'guidebook') raids on places of cultural note. Exeter, Norwich, York, Canterbury and Bath lost some of their heritage and, more importantly, some of their citizens. In his detailed telling of *The Blitz of Bath*, Martin Wainwright records how on 25 April 1942, fifty bombers took off from Nazi airfields in France. As they droned over Dorset, it was assumed they were making for the Bristol docks. In Bath, the citizens had become used to enemy planes flying overhead and, when the sirens went, many did not bother to take to the shelters. But this time the hatches opened and bombs fell both on Georgian buildings and also on Stothert & Pitt's engineering works where tank parts were made and human torpedoes were being developed. The planes returned the following night with bombs falling all over the city reaching out as far as the council estates of Twerton and Southdown. The damage was extensive and Wainwright estimates that over 80 per cent of the city was affected in some way. In all, nearly twenty thousand premises suffered some damage; 218 buildings of architectural and historical interest were destroyed and 417 people lost their lives.

Thereafter, bombing by piloted planes was virtually over.

British radar had become more efficient and, combined with the increasing night skills of British pilots, it meant that German planes experienced heavy losses. Perhaps most important, the *Luftwaffe* was increasingly diverted away to deal with the German war on the Soviet front.

In recent years, it has become fashionable to play down both the damage caused by the Blitz and the courage of its victims. Reports submitted to Mass Observation, and only subsequently published, have indicated that fear was widespread, that people fled, that looting took place. Angus Calder, in his *The Myth of the Blitz*, points out that people did grumble about rising prices, that shoppers were fed up with the queues, that bombed-out victims did have problems obtaining compensation, and that members of the armed forces were dissatisfied with their pay. Calder's theme is that it was essential for the British Government to create a picture of the plucky British people refusing to be put down by anything the Germans could throw at them. Consequently, newspaper reports, published photos, magazine articles and radio programmes were strictly controlled in order to prohibit any items which might undermine morale. Even wartime films like Noel Coward's *In Which We Serve* bolstered the 'we can take it' image. Hence, it is argued, the portrayal of the Blitz is partly a myth.

No doubt, the heroics were emphasized and the negatives played down by public reports. Yet the Blitz was a terrible ordeal as anyone who experienced it can testify. The bombs did slaughter thousands of people, some suddenly, others slowly and in great pain. Thousands more were cruelly injured and maimed. The high morale and the great courage of ordinary people, as Calder himself acknowledges, was not just a myth. The fact that so many people refused to be evacuated is an example of one kind of courage. Others are the workmen who repaired burning gasholders, the ARP who dragged out the injured from falling buildings, the firemen who risked—and lost—their lives amidst intense flames, the munition workers who insisted on making their way to their posts even when bombs were falling. This is truth.

An American, Dorothy Elmhirst, stayed in London for some weeks in 1941 and soon after she wrote the following, quoted in *Evacuees at Dartington* by Philip Connolly:

Perhaps the great glory of all these days was the organisation of the Civil Defence services—A.R.P.—A.F.S., rescue squads, ambulance units—first aid parties—stretcher bearers and so forth. Some of them were full time paid workers—others part time volunteers— but all showed the most extraordinary heroism, coolness and power of endurance. Every block in London is covered by these services—the moment a bomb falls they rush to the scene of action. A friend of mine told me that on one occasion, when a bomb fell in the house opposite hers, she rushed out into the street and already the A.R.P. workers were there. These workers are both men and women. Women drive the ambulances and act as wardens—often the head warden will be a woman. The rescue squads and fire fighters are men. They have to work in the dark with bombs dropping all round them— or worse still—if incendiaries have been dropped and a fire started they become an easy target for succeeding bombers. The task of the rescue squad is to dig out anyone who may have been buried under debris. They have to dig with their hands and fill baskets with rubble, which they pass along. They call for silence and strain to listen for any sounds that may come up through the great pile of debris—a groan—a cry—a whistle—a call—once the notes of a piano were heard and they worked for hours and hours until a small dog was uncovered lying along the keys. Sometimes these men work for twenty-four hours without ceasing—stopping only for a moment or two to swallow a cup of tea. On the morning after a raid you will see them scratching and digging—listening—digging again—often with relatives standing by—helplessly waiting—one of the most heartbreaking scenes one comes across. But often human beings are recovered—delivered from the certainty of that death—one of the many miracles.

The morning after a bad raid is hard to describe. The streets are a mess of broken glass and every few yards a building seems to have spilled itself into the street. The air is so thick with dust you can hardly breathe—and the smell of plaster and of gas seems to pervade the whole atmosphere. You try to pick your way down the street but often you have to turn back. Fire engines are still at work—you come suddenly into a street that is black with smoke—fires still burning. Demolition squads are already out on the job. I remember one lot of men in our own street looking hopelessly from one pile of debris to the next wondering where on earth to begin. I wondered how they had the courage to start all over again on a job that seemed never ending. But these people have some quality of dogged determination that nothing can down. And they have something else too that in adversity stands them in good stead—they can always make a joke. The ability to laugh in the moments of greatest strain and tension is peculiarly British I think—perhaps shared with Americans. You know the British tendency to understatement —well it serves them in good stead today. After a night when you felt you couldn't possibly live till the morning, the first people you meet on the stair or on the street will greet you with 'Noisy—wasn't it' or 'He gave us a packet didn't he'. He of course being Hitler. And their name for the Germans is typical again. 'There's Jerry—back again'. You see, half humorous—not allowing the Germans to frighten them by holding them in awe. And the official designation for a bombing is an 'incident'. At the A.R.P. post the telephone will ring and a voice says—'an incident in Queen Street'—that's all. Anyone who tends to make too much of their own misfortune is called a bomb bore. Friends of mine who have lost everything in the world they possess—everything save the clothes they stood in—just laughed and said—'Well, there are no possessions to worry about any more'. As Negly Farson, an American journalist said in his book 'You can't beat people who won't be beaten'. You should see the shops in London—battered—burned out—sometimes only the basement left—but a sign outside says 'open as usual'. The next door may be another shop with the windows all gone but a little notice 'more open than usual'. In one of the worst bombed sections of a great shopping street one chair had been left on a heap of rubble. Someone tied a label

on—'Reserved for victory parade'. And so it goes on—From the
North came a story of an old woman saying 'What does it matter
if Rome burns so long as we all keep fiddling'. And another—
'One good thing about this yere bombing—it makes you forget
the war'. Well, you see—not always logical but always good
humoured, brave and uncomplaining.

Other eye witnesses produce like accounts. It was not that fear did
not exist but rather that fear and courage co-existed in the same
people. I know that my parents were afraid of what the bombs might
do to their children and to themselves. Yet I know, too, that my
father was determined to keep up war production in the factory and
would not stay away from work or from the ARP even when a
splinter of metal in his eye caused him days of agony. I know that my
mother was prepared to endure most of the Blitz in order to keep the
family united. Theirs was the steady courage and determined
morale of ordinary, working-class people and it was repeated in
thousands of others. A Gallup poll taken at the height of the Blitz
revealed that 80 per cent of people were confident that Britain would
win the war. Indeed, the distinguished historian, A.J.P. Taylor,
concluded that the Blitz was:

a powerful solvent of class antagonism and ensured, too, that
there was none of the hostility between fighting men and
civilians which had characterised the first World War. The
fading of the Blitz inspired a mistaken feeling that Hitler had
shot his bolt, and English people believed that, by showing they
'could take it', they were already on the way to winning the war.

Truly it was a People's War and the Blitz was reality, not myth.

The trickle evacuation

The Blitz prompted another evacuation. But it was of a different
nature from that organized over three days in September 1939. It
occurred between the autumn of 1940 and the spring of 1942, as
evacuation followed the raids on different cities. Hence it earned
the title 'The Trickle Evacuation'.

This second evacuation was not within the phoney war. It was for real. Consequently, there was some panic. Following the initial Blitz on London crowds of people made for London's main-line stations and joined queues for trains going anywhere. So many evacuees from the East End of London made it to Oxford that the officials had to commandeer the Majestic Cinema—ironically advertising the film *Babes in The Wood*—and cram around six thousand people into a building designed for two thousand. In *The Children's War* Ruth Inglis tells of a mother who just turned up at Bury St Edmunds with five children and nowhere to go until the local vicar managed to find a dilapidated cottage.

Generally, however, the second evacuation was better organized than the first. Not only was it spread over a longer period but the officials could now draw upon their previous experience. Further, far fewer children went unaccompanied and more went with their mothers. Moreover, the reception areas, particularly the foster mothers and landladies were far more sympathetic to the evacuees who came with stories of how they were bombed out and how relatives and friends had been killed. The receiving officials and hostesses could now feel that they were making a contribution to the war. Not least, the Government hit upon the idea of the 'assisted evacuation scheme' in which financial assistance was given to those who found their own accommodation. In effect, two schemes were then in operation. In the first, the billeting officers found the foster homes or digs. In the second, the evacuees, usually the mothers, did so. This meant that the mothers had some choice over the homes to which they went. Between September 1940 and the end of 1941, the Government helped some 1,250,000 evacuees, mainly parents and children but also pregnant women, the elderly, blind, sick and homeless, to leave the bombed cities. To be sure, the competition for residences was intense as more and more cities were bombed and as more war factories and their staff were removed to safer areas. None the less, the second evacuation ran more smoothly than the first.

The trickle evacuation is less well documented than that of 1939. But a fascinating account was compiled for the pamphlet, *Evacuees at Dartington 1940–45*, edited by Philip Connolly. In the summer of 1940, four hundred children and their teachers left Gravesend in Kent and Southwark in London for Totnes in Devon They arrived earlier than expected so no reception committee was awaiting them. When the officials were hastily summoned, they found far more children than expected. They put most in temporary foster homes, with some hostesses taking twenty children while the remainder went to Dartington School, a progressive private school housed in the magnificent Dartington Hall. Its founders were Dorothy Elmhirst, daughter of an American millionaire, and her husband Leonard Elmhirst, a former distinguished colonial administrator. The pupils of the school had included the children of Bertrand Russell, Aldous Huxley and the Freuds. The Elmhirsts gladly accepted the evacuees, some of whom stayed permanently at the school, and Dorothy was continually involved. The experience is well described in a pamphlet by Margaret Stevens, one of the London teachers:

We were met at Totnes Station by Roger Morel, the Billeting Officer, who gave us the choice of being billeted in Totnes homes or together in the Ballet Jooss Dance School. Miss Hunter, our Headmistress, conferred with us and our unanimous decision was to remain together in view of the experience of our first evacuation.

On our arrival at Dartington Hall tired and hungry, we drew strength from the fact that we were at least together and given the quarters of the Ballet Jooss School—most of whom had been interned. Palliasses on the floor and a salad meal greeted us impressing the teachers, but causing many tears to the children. There are none so conservative as children and especially from deprived areas, as we were to learn. The salad for the most part remained untouched. Such food was unknown to them, and a bed was the most urgent wish. The parents had been given a list of suitable clothing including night attire in preparation for the evacuation. It was with some difficulty, but nevertheless implicit obedience by the children that day and night clothes were exchanged and seemingly the children were soon fast asleep.

From the Jooss Ballet School the teachers were then
escorted by K. Hall-Brown (HB) and Mrs Helen Elmhirst to
our rooms in the East Wing and to a meal in the White Hart.
Although so very exhausted, and by now it was dark, we felt we
had come to another planet—the total quiet, the slower pace
and total lack of evidence of war was bewildering. Looking up
at the moon through the Scots Pine by the Arts Department and
the very beautiful courtyard was truly overwhelming and
although so thankful for the sanctuary, nevertheless we had a
sense of guilt in remembering those we had left behind.
But the thought of the children soon snapped us back to
reality and with torches we went back to our charges to discover
the neatly folded clothes by each pillow had disappeared.
Turning back a few covers, we found they had been put on
again over the nightclothes. Later we were to learn 'T'aint
decent, miss, to go to bed without clofes on'.
Snatching a few hours sleep, the many problems of
adaptation to our new life had to be tackled. For several weeks
the great urns of porridge, potatoes and other vegetables, cooked
by Miss Hardwick in the White Hart Kitchen, had to be carried
across the lawns from the kitchen to the school. Once again
walking the country lanes, as in the first evacuation, was the
main source of our education, for we were without any kind of
teaching equipment and, mercifully, the weather befriended us.
During the initial period there was little contact with the
courtyard residents. We were so busy, hardly taking time to eat
in the White Hart and never indulging in coffee in the Solar.
We were bewildered with so much to do, and although teaching
in State Schools meant being responsible for 48 children in a
class, we now looked after their well-being for 24 hours each
day. A responsibility in loco parentis which seemed to horrify
those who were used to the luxury and educational advantage
of small classes. (Average size of class at Dartington Hall
School was about 10–12.)

The organization of the second evacuation remained in the
hands of local authorities such as the officials at Gravesend and

Totnes. But by this time the Ministry of Health had sent in advisers to help them. Lucy Faithfull was appointed a regional welfare officer and sent to the Midlands (of which more in the next chapter). Her boss at the Ministry was Geraldine Aves who gave the regional officers excellent support and who in after years played an important part in the development of social work in Britain. In 1941 she transferred Lucy to the West Country again in the role of advising officials about evacuation policy and practice and acting as a link between them and Government. However, she became much more involved as a kind of trouble-shooter. She explained to me:

> I was sent to Plymouth to help the evacuation there into Devon and Cornwall. I stayed in Plymouth for most of the rest of the war, where I was the regional welfare officer—and I was given a car. I only had one night of bombing in Plymouth but it was a terrible night. I thought my last hours had come. I was staying at the Settlement and a bomb fell just up the road so that the whole place was shaken and the lights fell in. Devon and Cornwall already had a large number of evacuee children from London but now children had to be moved out of Plymouth. Then London had another terrible night of bombing and yet more places had to be found. I went to the clerk of the council in Truro and told him the Ministry had asked me to find billets in Truro for about 400 children. He said he could do nothing without asking the rural district council. I told him that bombed-out children in London were waiting in schools. He agreed to call a meeting of the council that night and I went to it and told them that the Minister of Health would appreciate it if they would take the children at once. They said, 'But we don't know you. We've never met you before. We can't give you an answer straightaway.' They told me to come back the next night and this time they agreed. The billeting officer already had the names of prospective foster homes so we could then act quickly. It was just a matter of getting official permission.
>
> I also had problems in Ilfracombe where people just refused to take any foster children. The children had arrived and were

*staying in schools looked after by teachers and volunteers. I
had to live in Ilfracombe for three months and eventually, by
visiting and persuasion got them to change their minds. And it
worked out well.*

*I was also responsible for a number of old people who were
evacuated. We requisitioned a very prestigious hotel and used it
for forty to fifty old people. A town clerk phoned me to say he
had a terrible problem. The billeting officer could not find
anywhere for an old lady, who was a lavatory cleaner in London,
who was absolutely filthy, crawling. I rang up the matron at the
hotel and said, 'You must take her but have a bath ready.' I
picked up the old lady and told her she would have to have a
bath. "I've never had a bath," she said, "And I'm not going to
start now." I stopped the car and told her that if she would not
have a bath then I would leave her at the gate. So she agreed.
When we arrived, matron whisked her upstairs to the bathroom.
She was amazed to see her whip off a wig with the words, "The
young lady said I must wash from top to toe". So she washed
herself and her wig.*

*She was in a room with a balcony. Suddenly we heard this
terrible scream and rushed upstairs. She had hung her wig on
the balcony to dry and a seagull had swooped and flown off
with it. There she was as bald as a coot. I fetched my hat and
put it on her. She looked rather nice. It took me six months to
get the money out of the Ministry to replace her wig.*

Evacuation was also to be my lot again. Our parents were reluctant to be parted but Ilford was receiving its share of bombs. It took
thirty-seven parachute mines, 968 high explosive bombs and
thousands of incendiary bombs. Inevitably some were close to us.
The Co-op shop not far away in the High Road was obliterated by a
direct hit. Our windows and tiles were blasted. Reluctantly, it was
agreed again that Dad must stay while Mum, my sister and I
departed. We went initially to Brentwood where her sister,
husband (a gas worker) and children lived. Uncle kept rabbits and
my main memory is of eating rabbit stew. He even swallowed their
eyes. Brentwood was an ideal location for us in that it was removed

from the docks and factories which were the target of the bombers yet was sufficiently near for Dad to visit. When he made it in an evening, both families would go to a working man's social club where they participated in table tennis, dancing, singing and two things our dad particularly liked—darts and corny jokes. But Auntie and Uncle's council house was far too small even for their needs so we had to move again.

We made the short trip to the village of Heronsgate to the home of our great-aunt. She was a daunting woman, a staunch church-goer who even had her own organ. She also had a walking stick which she banged fiercely on the floorboards to frighten the rats against whom she waged war. Her home was beside a pond, cov-ered in green slime, an old wooden school which Dad had attended as a small boy, and close to fields with long grass where we used to race around. These rural attractions were somewhat out-weighed, in my estimation, by a lack of running water, by a smelly toilet at the bottom of the garden which was emptied once a week, and a single tap outside the house. This placement, our fourth with relatives, also broke down.

We came home briefly but not for long. So far we had been evacuated with the officially organized Government scheme, with private arrangements made with our relatives, and then, to complete the hat trick, we participated in the Government assisted scheme and so found ourselves in Cranleigh, Kent. Cranleigh could not have been entirely safe for, in her autobiography, Lady Allen of Hurt-wood, who lived there, described enemy planes machine-gunning local shops and German bombers crashing in the fields. None the less, it was a lot safer than Ilford. It was now the autumn of 1941 and I started school. Clutching my gas mask and my sister's hand, I made what seemed the long walk to school. The school consisted of a large, single, crowded, noisy, hall. Each class sat around a table just a few feet from the next class. I recall trying to copy the letters of the alphabet. I took a dislike to school, except for the break when we got free milk with a straw.

The stay in Cranleigh lasted over a year then we moved yet again—I never fully understood the reasons. We were back in Ilford for a short stay then off on the longest trip yet to a tiny hamlet called Cross Keys, a few miles outside Hereford. We were billetted in one of a row of four farm labourer's cottages. Once more it was the toilet in the garden and the water heated upon the stove but these were halcyon days for me. The country school was miles away and Mum just refused to make us walk to it despite the calls and threats from the truancy officer.

I was now old enough to roam the fields and lanes with the local kids and a few other evacuees. We had a den up in a huge tree and another one under a road bridge. They took me on my first scrumping expedition. Our little band crept into a farmer's orchard, flitting from tree to tree like commandos. We stuffed the apples into our short-sleeved pullovers by drawing up the lower end into a kind of bag. 'Farmer's coming!' went up the cry. The gang fled. As the youngest and slowest, I brought up the rear of the retreat as the farmer gave chase, waving a stick and threatening what he was going to do to us. It was me or the apples and, reluctantly, I let my load go in order to make good my escape. Later, the gang shared one with me as we re-lived our adventure under the bridge. As we walked the country lanes, we sometimes saw prisoners of war—I think they were Italian—working in the fields and they would wave and laugh with us. I can remember pondering that if these men were so nice, why were we fighting them?

One family of evacuees, also from Ilford, were billetted on a large farm. The farmer there used to let us kids in to watch and once he taught me how to carry a live chicken by its legs. Then came the excitement of harvest and I can still envisage the yellow corn and the arrival of the combine harvester as it went from farm to farm. We even went to the harvest festival auction in the local church hall. Seeing that goods were obtained by people raising their hand and shouting out, I did the same when some flowers were held up which I thought just right for Mum. It was explained to me that I had to have money to get the goods but, at least, it gave everyone a good laugh.

I wish I could have afforded those flowers for Mum. How she loved, cared and battled for us. Sometimes we all went to the local pub in the evening where we sat outside on a bench and Mum brought us Tizer and crisps. She was always popping out to see that we were all right. Occasionally we had the special treat of catching the country bus into a nearby town. I remember visiting Hereford where we sat on concrete blocks to eat our fish and chips. We then went to a huge cinema and during the film the song 'Lili Marlene' was sung. I could not understand it properly but I knew it was about the separation of lovers. And I knew that Mum missed Dad. Now and then Dad did manage the long trip to Cross Keys. Once he drove a large, old-fashioned lorry. How he got it, and the petrol, I'll never know. My young heart used to jump when he arrived and Mum rushed out to him. They would stroll arm in arm down the lanes with us kids a few feet behind. They would sometimes have a fag, Players for Dad and Craven A cork-tipped for Mum. Once I picked up a fag end which dad had thrown away and had a few puffs. He cuffed me and I have never smoked since. Today I can't hear 'Lili Marlene' without thinking of them.

The only fly in our evacuee ointment was the householder at the cottage. He was a large, burly, farm labourer who ruled his kindly wife with physical and verbal violence. Our mum was not the type to be brow-beaten by anyone—perhaps that was why we moved around so much—especially when her children were involved. One morning he accused me of stealing his tomatoes which had been ripening on the window sill and indicated that he wanted to punish me. Mum retorted that if anyone was going to punish me it would be her and, besides, I hadn't taken the tomatoes, it was the rats. He replied that rats gnawed tomatoes, not removed them altogether. Good point, so perhaps I was guilty. Mum avoided his reaction by promptly gathering us together and walking out.

We made our way back to Ilford, joining thousands of other returning evacuees. Home again.

3 The Doodle-bug Evacuation

During 1943, occasional enemy raids still occurred. On 20 June, a school in Catford, south-east London, suffered a direct daylight hit. It contained some pupils who had returned from evacuation and thirty-eight children and six adults were killed.

Such a tragedy, however, could not dampen the belief that the Blitz had failed, that the tide had turned, that the allies were winning the war. In North Africa, Rommel was in retreat from Montgomery. In the Atlantic, British and American destroyers were finally countering the U-boats and imports of raw materials to Britain were increasing. From bases in eastern England, bombers took the offensive against Germany and from March 1943 wreaked terrible damage on enemy cities. In July, Allied forces landed in Sicily and began to move into Italy. The following year, preparations were made for the Allied offensive in France with D-Day occurring on 6 June 1944. On that day, I stood on our coal-box and watched a seemingly endless flow of planes spearing towards Europe.

I am not sure when we arrived back in Ilford. Probably it was the autumn of 1943. Certainly I was attending South Park school in the last months of the year. In November, Nan came to look after us. One day, as I came in from school, she said, 'There's a lovely surprise for you, guess what it is.' I replied, 'Fish and chips.' She burst out laughing. The surprise was a baby brother, John.

Aged seven, I used to walk to school with my sister and with a cousin who, for some reason, was temporarily staying with us. We walked alongside the park, with all its railings taken for the war effort, looking at bomb sites. I always had an old tennis ball at my feet which I dribbled in the gutters and then threw against the sides of houses. Following in my dad's footsteps I was already football crazy. At the weekends and when the lighter evenings came in 1944, I would roam around with my mates. Just over the road from our house was a huge dump where bomb debris was piled. There we ran, climbed and chased for hours. Next to our house was a transport drivers' cafe where my dad often went for a cup of tea and a laugh. Sometimes he took me with him and I enjoyed the banter of the army and civilian drivers. The cafe did not have chairs but what can only be described as high-backed pews. The men would pass me over their heads to a vacant space and buy me a glass of Tizer and, now and then, the owner would present me with his speciality— frozen custard.

But the freedom of roaming and the freedom from fear was about to end again. A few weeks after D-Day, explosions took place in several parts of southern England. They had been preceded by a low drone and spluttering noises, like a car running out of petrol, in the sky. Initially, the Government restricted news and the BBC referred simply to 'activity over southern England'. Soon the Government had to concede that the Germans were recommencing attacks on Britain with pilot-less planes. The V1s, as they were officially called, were small planes, without a pilot, which were packed with explosives and launched from pads in France with just enough petrol to reach Britain. Once the fuel ran out, they crashed. Herbert Morrison, who had been Home Secretary since 1942, tried to play down the devastating effects of the new weapons by issuing reports that they were falling harmlessly into fields. But the planes and their explosions could be seen and heard and felt in the urban areas. Soon a hundred attacks a day were coming. London was the main target. Angus Calder in *The People's War* well describes them:

The fiery tails of the little planes, seen sharply at night travelling at great speed across the skies, had prompted cheering at first, when people had taken them for enemy fighters in flames. But soon they were all too easily recognized. There was the noise, variously described as 'a grating, sinister growl which increased as it approached to a most menacing roar'; a 'disagreeable splutter, like an aerial motor bicycle in bad running order'; and 'a terrific noise like an express train with a curious hidden undertone'. They were christened 'doodle bugs' or 'buzz bombs'; as the doodling or buzzing grew louder, those below waited tensely in case the engine cut out. When the V1 ran out of fuel it crashed to earth with a deep-throated roar, followed by a blinding flash and a tall, sooty plume of smoke. If the noise seemed to stop directly above them, people flung themselves on the floor, under the table, into doorways. Work, meetings, parties, sleep were subject to hectic interruptions; not the least of the Londoner's grudges against the buzz bombs was that they deprived him of dignity. Sometimes, however, they dived straight to earth without their engines cutting out; there was nothing one could do about that.

Ilford became an early target. An air raid warden was enjoying a bath when a huge explosion shattered most of his home but left him unhurt. He rushed out to find that a doodle-bug had come down nearby. Soon the attacks were more lethal. Two young nurses and seven patients were killed when one hit a hospital in the grounds of Dr Barnardo's Homes: over one hundred children nearby escaped. A fourteen-year-old girl was killed while visiting a friend's home. Three brothers were searching for possessions in their home which had been damaged two days before when another buzz bomb landed and killed them. The doodle-bugs were not easy to spot in cloudy weather and that summer was a wet one. For eighty days, people listened intently and then ran, shouting warnings, if they heard or saw one. In all, fifty-seven landed on Ilford, killing sixty-nine residents and injuring another 644. It is recorded that 1,631 homes were destroyed and 24,000 damaged. Extra wardens had to be drafted in from the Midlands to help with digging out the injured. Many people were made homeless until council workmen could fix tarpaulins onto damaged roofs and repair walls.

Our family frequently heard explosions and saw the buzz bombs. On 16 June, one fell a couple of hundred yards away. Our home suffered a few broken windows and lost some slates. Others lost everything and a couple moved in with us. The man was a stamp collecting enthusiast and started me off on this hobby with a number of stamps. They did not stay long for soon we were to be temporarily homeless as well.

At the end of June, my sister and I had been sent on an errand to the green-grocer's shop just over the road. Suddenly, in the distance, we spotted a doodle-bug, getting ever nearer. Its engine cut and it began its descent directly towards us. I just watched the plane, transfixed to the spot. It passed low over the houses opposite as somebody dragged me down to the floor. It landed with a tremendous explosion, throwing glass, bricks and rubble everywhere. A whole row of houses was flattened—they stayed in ruins for years. Then our distraught mum came running over to find us.

Our home had been damaged. Dad and Mum still resisted evacuation and we moved in with Nan and Grandad. We were a close-knit family with grand-parents, aunts and uncles who saw each other frequently. So I welcomed the move to their home. Nan was homely and motherly. She used to tell me tales about when she had been a maid in service and had to iron the master's morning newspaper so that there were no creases in it. And she was a good cook. Grandad was a character, a bookies' runner, full of stories about the races and tips for winners. They shared the home with an aunt and uncle, the latter being abroad in the army, but they immediately took us in. They had a Morrison shelter which filled their front room. Made of steel with wire mesh on all sides, it was two feet nine inches tall. Mum, my sister, my baby brother and I slept in it every night and dashed in when doodle-bugs were around. I never considered then that our relatives were endangering themselves by making room for us. But, within a few weeks, our house was repaired and we moved back.

Ilford was just one part of London. Croydon, which was in the bombers' flight path to London, suffered even more severely—142 doodle-bugs. In Central London, a V1 scored a direct hit on the Guard's Chapel during a service so that 119 people were killed and

102 seriously injured. The doodle-bugs reached as far as Oldham where twenty-seven people lost their lives; but the main concentration was on London and south-east England. In all about 600 civilians lost their lives and over 16,000 were badly wounded.

One of the difficulties in stopping the flying bombs was that, even when hit in the air, the subsequent explosion could still cause considerable damage below. Consequently, the ack-ack guns were moved from London to the coast so that increasingly the incoming doodle-bugs were shot down over the sea. The menace, however, was not completely stopped until Allied troops captured their launching pads in northern France.

The V2s

In September, Duncan Sandys MP, who was now in charge of defensive operations, signalled the decline of the V1s by announcing 'The Battle of London is over.' He could not have been more wrong. A day later, London was shattered by even greater explosions. The Government pretended they were gas explosions. The Londoners knew they were the next German weapon and referred to the flashes of white light as 'flying gas mains'. Eventually the Government had to concede they were the V2s, rockets some 45 feet long and weighing 14 tons, which sped from their bases in Holland.

Bomber planes could be spotted and warnings given by sirens. V1s could usually be seen, even if only at the last moment, and a dash made for shelter. The worst aspect of the V2 rockets was that they made virtually no sound and fell without warning. Ack-ack guns and fighter planes could not stop them. There was no defence. They were more terrifying and more destructive than any previous weapon. In one London borough, four V2s severely damaged over 2,000 houses. In all 500 were to hit London and 600 elsewhere. The death toll was grim—2,274 people lost their lives and over 6,000 people were seriously wounded.

It was then that Herbert Morrison opened up the deep tube shelters. In order to avoid over-crowding, and a repetition of a panic which had crushed a number of people to death, entry was by ticket only. The trouble was that no one could be sure about when to go as no sirens could give warning against V2s. Some Londoners opted to use the tube shelters as home, sleeping there and emerging to go to their jobs. But such an option was not open to those who did not live near the tubes and could hardly be fitted in with the lives of mothers with young children. The same agonizing decisions were being faced again: should the children be evacuated?

Although Ilford suffered many attacks—forty-nine rockets in all—our parents were determined to keep the family together and to resist evacuation. Initially, Mum tried to get us to live in our shelter. She would emerge to shop and cook meals which she then brought down to us. It proved impossible. My sister and I could not be confined to a small space for such long periods. The baby constantly had to be brought up for washing, changing and fresh air. So the shelter life was abandoned. However, Mum did get a much tighter rein on us and I was not allowed to roam around with my friends.

We still went to school but, once home, I was not allowed out on my own. Meal times became more important. We always had our evening meal sitting at the table and I used to listen to our parents' conversations. Mum would recount how she had persuaded the butcher to give her a little extra Spam and, while at the clinic collecting the dried milk and orange juice, a friend had told her that the meat was being mixed with horse meat. Dad would talk about the factory and the ARP and sometimes tell us about bananas and oranges which we never saw. One batch of oranges had reached Ilford and provoked a mini-riot with the greengrocer having to summon police protection from housewives. We never got any.

After the meal, we would fuss around the baby, taking turns to cuddle him and help him stand up. He had an enormous gas mask which seemed to fit all around him and which was operated with a hand pump. I had long given up carrying my gas mask although Dad, as a conscientious warden, still carried his. Then I would peep through the curtains. The black-out was still in operation although it could not have been much protection against V2s. A few years later I became an avid reader of Richmal Crompton's *Just William* books and discovered that, in the black-out, his gang, called the Outlaws, had:

roamed the countryside unhindered in its thrilling new
unlightened condition. They formed bands and tracked each
other down. They occasionally leapt out from behind trees to
terrify nervous pedestrians, they pushed each other into ditches,
they narrowly missed being run over several times at night and
had given heart attacks to innumerable motorists.

This paragraph surprised me for I could not understand how
William's parents had let him out during the black-out. But I
could not go out and often took comfort in listening to the radio.
Large, brown and polished, the radio stood high on a shelf out of
my reach. I was sent to get its batteries re-filled, I think they were
called accumulators. At this stage, Dad would not have the radio
on during meal times but afterwards it was an important part of
our lives. We listened to the news to obtain information about the
progress of the war. And it was our source of entertainment. Dad
was out a lot on his ARP duties but, when home, I loved it when we
listened, sang along and laughed as a family.

Dad thought Vera Lynn was marvellous and, in later years, the
sound of her voice would always move him deeply. Mum liked
Hutch—Leslie Hutchinson—a West Indian who had established
himself as a night club singer. A lunch-time programme, repeated in
the evenings, was Break for Music when ENSA staff, Entertainments
National Service Association, visited factories. In 1944 it broadcast
from Plessey's, where Dad worked. But the national favourite was
undoubtedly ITMA which attracted an audience of 16 million
listeners. As an eight-year-old, it was not the quick fire Tommy
Handley but rather the various characters with their catch-phrases
which made me laugh. Mrs Mopp, Mona Lott, and my favourite,
Colonel Chinstrap with his 'I don't mind if I do', became our catch-
phrases: 'Some more corned beef, Bob?' 'I don't mind if I do' I would
answer. It was always certain to raise a chuckle. After the radio, we
might play cards together. Gathering around the kitchen table we
would play knockout, snap and 'beat your neighbours out of doors'. I
was a bad loser and often got told off for sulking.

We did continue one outing. The Ilford Hippodrome, the local
variety theatre, sometimes pasted a poster on our fence for which

Dad received a couple of free tickets. Rockets or no rockets, we still went. When it was my occasional turn, I loved it: the crowded theatre, the smoky atmosphere, the live performances, the community singing, the sense of defiance that we would continue to enjoy ourselves despite the danger, and all the jokes against Hitler. I can recall trapeze artists, dancers and acrobats with two performers remembered by name. One was the world champion table tennis player, Victor Barna, who played on stage with the English champion, Alec Brook. The bald-headed Barna won the games with ease. Brook would slam the ball over the net with Barna retreating and still returning it until he was out of sight in the wings with the ball still coming back to frustrate Brook. The other was Teddy Brown, billed as 'the world's greatest xylophonist'. Brown was exceedingly fat yet nimbly jumped around the stage as he played brilliantly. Soon after, the Hippodrome did receive a direct hit from a V2 and was destroyed for good.

Such treats were rare interludes. For the first time in the war, I possessed a sense of likely death. Previously, I had always considered that we would get to, and be safe in, our shelter. Now I understood that the V2s gave no warning and could not be stopped. I had my first thoughts of what happened, if anything, after death. There was a cemetery near our home and sometimes I used to see the burials taking place. Once, I am not sure if it was then or later, I asked Mum what happened when we died. She told me not to worry about such things.

On 24 November 1944 I was in school when it was rocked by an enormous explosion. Some windows caved in. We all knew that another V2 had come down. Teachers held whispered conversations and then we were told to go home. Looking back, I am amazed that small children were sent back alone but, I suppose, the teachers were anxious to see what had happened to their families and homes. I walked alone. South Park Crescent was a wreck. My pal, Billy, stood there. 'My mum and dad have been killed,' he announced. In fact, they were still alive although he did not know that. I walked on with fear in my heart. I stopped in astonishment at the entrance to the park. A huge clock tower, a famous local landmark, had stood there. Now it was completely gone and replaced by a huge crater where the V2 had hit it. Our home was eighty yards away.

The street was chaotic, with vehicles, no doubt parked for the cafe, strewn all over the place. Strangely enough, the post-box was still standing, although it had holes in it (they are still there today). Our fence was down and, looking up, I could see into my sister's bedroom where the wall had been blown in. I clambered over rubble to the hole where the back door had been. I knew that my sister had been at her school but I was frightened for the others. 'Mum, Dad,' I yelled tearfully. I searched for them under remains of furniture and then climbed the crumbling stairs. Upstairs my feet kicked plaster which sent more dust swirling around. The boxroom where I slept and the front bedroom were more or less intact but empty. The back of the house was torn apart. I stumbled into my sister's room and looked out of the space where the wall had been. The remains of her toys were blown into a pile. I could not make out her bed at all. Tears flowed as I reasoned that no one could have been here and lived. Despair. I remember thinking, 'What do I do now? Where do I go?' I was about to make my way to Nan's when I felt a hand on my shoulder. 'It's all right, son.' It was Dad.

Later I was told that Mum had been peeling potatoes at the sink when the explosion came. She was injured and had to be dug out. As she was carried to the ambulance, she called out that her baby was still in the home. A man, we never knew his name, returned to dig and found baby John under a door with debris piled on it. Almost certainly the door saved his life. It was his first birthday. Dad had rushed back from the factory and went to the hospital before coming to find me.

My mother and brother were fortunate, for all around them other people lost their lives. Mr and Mrs Russell were a familiar, elderly, couple who pushed around a barrow to sell and deliver vegetables and fruit. They were directly outside our house when the rocket fell. Mr Russell was killed instantly while his wife lost her legs. A neighbour was killed as was a building worker, whom we did not know, who was unlucky enough to be walking by at that moment. Over the road was a family where the soldier son had come to spend his leave with his wife and mother. The wife had just slipped out for some shopping and lived. The soldier and his mother were killed in the house. There were many injuries. Astonishingly, nobody was killed in the cafe and it may have been that the lorries parked outside took the full force of the blast. Dad, my sister and myself moved into Nan's again. This time the danger had been too close. When mum and my brother were discharged from hospital dad sent us away. Evacuation again.

The third evacuation

By this time, the evacuation had been under way for months. The doodle-bugs had stimulated a third wave. Some hospitals went first. John Vaizey was a teenager and long-term patient in a hospital just north of London. In *Scenes from Institutional Life* he wrote:

The summer term wore on and Whitsun came in a blaze of sunshine. On June 6th the allied armies landed in Normandy; then towards the end of the month, as we were waking up, a puffing aeroplane passed by, flames pouring from its tail. This was the first V1 we saw; in the days that followed there were many more, and we were no longer put into the courtyard. For three weeks there were fairly frequent explosions. In one of them Staff Nurse J. was killed. There was a decision to evacuate the hospital to the west of England ...

The shaky lorries and a fleet of ambulances took the whole hospital to ambulance trains at H. station, at five o'clock on a July morning. We were loaded on tiers of bunks. Hospital trains have no windows, and are lit by the hard bright light that underground trains have. For fifteen hours the train rocked on through England. We had no idea where we were going; even the medical staff were kept in ignorance. The passion for secrecy that characterized the war, the medical profession and the authorities was here combined in a silliness without reason. The train steamed on, until at eight o'clock at night we were unloaded into ARP vans at a goods station in S. A winding ascending road took us to a prefabricated military hospital on a hillside among trees.

In July, the evacuation gathered pace elsewhere. The evacuees were mainly but not wholly from London. The official scheme arranged for 307,600 evacuees while another 550,000 went under the assisted scheme. Taking into account those who had not returned from the two previous evacuations, by July well over a million people, mainly school children, young children and mothers, were in evacuation. In Ilford, July witnessed 1,325 unaccompanied children and 1,570 children with mothers leaving with the official scheme. The authorities expressed disappointment that there were not more. They went mainly to destinations in the north of England, particularly Macclesfield, Barnoldswick, Halifax, Bolton, Wake-field, Kendal and Accrington. Another 5,200 received travel warrants and promise of allowances under the assisted scheme. Interestingly, some returned to billets where they had earlier lived during the previous two official schemes.

The Ilford Recorder gave most attention to what happened at Accrington where reception officials had gathered at the station having made arrangements to board school children from Ilford. Due to a muddle, the school children finished up in Oldham while a party of mothers with young children got out at Accrington. The billeting officers then had some difficulties in finding places for them. Eventually they succeeded and the Ilford paper was full of praise for their efforts and pointed out that the Accrington medical officer of health had gone out of his way to say that the children were clean and well cared-for—which pleased the Ilford mothers. He also opened all clinics to evacuee families. However, some families were not immediately found billets and were put together into rest centres which had not been prepared for them. The paper's reporter interviewed a number of these mothers and published their words:

We were told several times that we would not be long and several times our cases were put in a bus and taken out again. By degrees, people with only one child got billets. In the afternoon, some of the women were taken in a bus, and they told us afterwards that they were taken around looking for billets, and that some of the people would not open the doors to them.

I went out for a few minutes to a shop and one of the local women stopped me and said she was very sorry for us. There were other people who cried and gave us milk, and said they were sorry for us. They could not take us because they had only very small cottages.

About 6.30 that evening some of us decided that we would come home. We had had a midday meal of stew and rice and also tea. They asked us to stay, and said they would make people take us, but we did not want to go to people who were made to take us. We came back during the night. We had to pay our own fares back.

For a month *The Ilford Recorder* continued with stories about happy evacuees just as it had done during the previous two evacuations. Then it expressed alarm that evacuees were returning home too quickly so that by September over 30 per cent were back in Ilford. It condemned Duncan Sandys' September statement that the air attacks were over as premature. The paper proved wiser than Sandys, for soon came the V2s which led to yet another wave of evacuation. It was soon after this that I was evacuated with my mother, sister and brother to Hastings.

Hastings may seem a strange place for evacuation, being so near to France. But, by this time, there was no prospect of invasion and any rockets flew overhead on their way to London. We were lodged in Emmanuel Road. 'Squeezed in' is a more appropriate word, for all four of us were in one upstairs room which served as bedroom, kitchen and living quarters. But we were safe and together. I started at another school. My sister walked with me and then went to another part of it. At the first break, I stood alone in the playground and watched several boys and girls line up for a severe caning from a teacher. It was a strict and hard school. The classrooms were crowded, I was behind in all subjects, and, for the first time, I experienced anti-evacuee feeling. The 'vaccees' and the local children did not mix and we were blamed for the densely-packed classrooms. I had not been evacuated as part of a school unit so had no teachers whom I knew. It seemed to me that the teachers were quick to blame and punish the Londoners. I was miserable in school, embarrassed by my educational backwardness and cowed by the harsh attitudes. I longed for the bell at the end of the day.

Outside school, I enjoyed Hastings. As a family, with my sister, or alone, I explored the cliffs and stony beaches and played amongst the machine-gun boxes and tank barriers. I watched the fishermen washing their nets and I loved 'bottle alley' in St Leonard's—a promenade with coloured glass cemented into its walls. I loved to feel the wind against my cheeks on the high cliffs. Once the strong winds ripped a woman's hat off her head, I think she had just come out of church, and I chased it for her. Unfortunately, in stopping it I put my foot through it and, instead of being grateful, she gave me a shaking. Then there was the castle and the caves. Both were closed to the public in war-time but they stimulated my boyish imagination to make up stories about Norman soldiers, King Harold, and smugglers. In the winter, I was fascinated by the size of the waves and the height of the spray as the tide pounded against the rocks. I used to play running in as the waves rose and then dodging back as they fell—until Mum ordered me away. In 1945 we came home for the final time. The war was definitely over.

The return

The Government had been drawing up plans for the return of the evacuees since 1943. Of course, many came home under their own steam and choosing. None the less, in September 1944, even though some people were still fleeing from the V2s, the Ministry of Health began to finalize its operations. One decision was straightforward— London evacuees would be the last to come home as the capital was still the subject of air attack. The arrangements were not easy. Many cities' children were scattered over a multitude of evacuation locations. Children from the London County Council were evacuated to over one thousand different places. Within the reception zones, officials had to make house to house investigations to establish just how many unaccompanied children were still there. Then they had to link with the evacuation zones to ensure whether their parents were still there and whether they were in a position to take them back. In a number of cases, the parents were homeless due to bombing. In more tragic ones, both parents had been killed or could not be traced. The investigations were swiftly made and in September and October 1944, the signal was given for evacuees from the north-western areas of England to go home. This was followed by those from other northern cities and then from the Midlands and Scotland. By the end of the year, only evacuees from London and East Coast towns were still away.

Early in 1945, the Allied armies captured the V2 bases in Holland and the return of the 425,000 Londoners got under way. On 2 May 1945, two days after the death of Hitler, the official go-ahead for the remaining evacuees was given. The arrangements entailed 115 special trains to carry 29,701 unaccompanied children, 21,127 mothers with children and 3,489 other adults. In addition, thousands travelled separately with travel vouchers or at their own expense. The organization was so complex that many had to celebrate VE Day on 8 May at their evacuation locations. It was officially declared complete by 12 July, although numbers remained behind either because their parents were unable to take them or because contact had been lost.

Thanksgiving

Whether back home or still away, the evacuees joined the rest of the nation in celebrations to mark victory, if not the complete end of the war. *The Daily Mirror*, which my parents sometimes read, marked the occasion by finally presenting their famous strip cartoon character, Jane, in her birthday suit. Revellers thronged to Trafalgar Square and outside Buckingham Palace. Those at home tuned in to Winston Churchill on the radio. And all day, whether in St Paul's Cathedral, village churches or small urban chapels, worshippers flooded in for services of thanksgiving to God for victory and preservation.

Was evacuation also a cause for thanksgiving? After all, it tore many children away from their parents. It was: for two reasons. First, evacuation did save lives. It is true that some did lose their lives while on evacuation. Enemy planes returning after raids occasionally ditched unused bombs anywhere. In Totnes, a school and railway station were machine-gunned, by a plane, for no apparent reason. But these were exceptions. Generally, evacuees were safe. Indeed, throughout Britain only 7,736 children were killed by bomb attacks. Every one was the loss of a precious, valuable life but the number is small compared with the killing power of the bombers, the V1s and the V2s, and small compared with the numbers who died under Allied bombs. Evacuation did succeed in moving many children away from danger zones and therefore preserved many lives.

Second, evacuation was carried out in such a way that many small children stayed with their mothers while most older ones lived in private homes. The Government resisted calls to house evacuees in large camps or institutions and thereby ensured that they experienced something of family life. As Richard Titmuss in *Problems of Social Policy* explained:

> *the situation of these evacuated children in private households was immensely better, when viewed as a whole, than that of the 80,000 or so children who, deprived of a normal home life, were being brought up in the coldly isolated world of charitable homes and Poor Law institutions.*

If the evacuation did give grounds for thanksgiving then many of the thanks should be expressed to women. Although men still held the majority of senior posts in statutory and voluntary national bodies, it was mainly women who gathered the evacuees together, accompanied them on trains, met them at reception, found them billets, looked after them in foster homes and taught them in schools. And it was mothers who stuck with their small children, be it during the Blitz under the threat of bombs or in lodgings in isolated villages. It was women who received the dreaded official notifications that their husbands had been killed in action and who yet continued to build a life for their children.

Mary Clayton's husband was in a POW camp. She moved to various evacuation locations while looking after their son, often with little money and in poor accommodation. Eventually her husband came home and later, in her diary, she wrote (quoted in *War Wives*):

I now realize just how much hope and faith I'd put into prayer and how I'd trusted that God would take care of my dear ones for me. Bobby, my son, and Sammy, my husband, are still as precious to me even after all these years.

She thanked God and so do I. I also want to thank all these brave and loving women, one of whom was my mother.

4 The Experience of Evacuation

In 1939, as many as 1,400,000 people were moved under Government evacuation schemes. Thereafter evacuees criss-crossed between the danger and reception zones so that even the Government historian Professor Titmuss could not be sure of numbers. He did estimate that by August 1940 the number of official evacuees was only 546,000, but that numbers rose again to 1,368,780 by February 1941 then steadily declined, until 1944 when numbers rose again to over one million. In all, he reckons that four million people participated in the combined Government inspired evacuations, the direct provision and the assisted schemes. In addition, some two million people made private arrangements and, taking account of those who went abroad and the elderly who were removed, some estimates reach a total of eight million evacuees.

Such massive movement of population must have had some effects on the participants. In the last chapter it was argued that evacuation did succeed in saving lives and did so while still keeping most evacuees within a family framework. But this is not to say that the participants always enjoyed or benefited from it socially, emotionally and educationally. What was the evacuation experience like for the foster parents, the mothers, the children?

The priority of getting children to safety allowed no time or resources to set in motion a nationwide investigation into its effects. Afterwards the majority of evacuees did not write about their own reactions. The evidence is incomplete. None the less, the drama of evacuation did prompt some to write about their feelings and I have been able to interview a number of participants. At the time, a small but important number of books recorded observations about the events, and a valuable study—Susan Issacs' *The Cambridge Evacuation Survey*—was made of evacuation in Cambridge. Most important, the Government commissioned Richard Titmuss to compile his massive civil history of the period—*Problems of Social Policy*, published in 1950. Incomplete though the evidence is, I hope it is sufficient to allow me to portray the experiences of those at the hard end of evacuation.

The foster parents

The term 'foster parents' is usually applied to persons who have taken on the role of substitute parents by choice. Taking in evacuees was often imposed upon householders. In theory, they could have been prosecuted for refusing to co-operate. It rarely if ever came to that but when billeting officers knocked on doors and asked how many rooms were empty it was assumed that evacuees would be taken in unless good reasons could be put forward for not doing so. Certainly, the initial welcome in September 1939 to the exhausted children and mothers was usually friendly enough, but an underlying feeling of resentment and imposition soon burst into a torrent of complaints. The valuable study of evacuation made by the Women's Group On Public Welfare—*Our Towns: A Close-up* commented:

> *hardly had billeting been completed when complaints arose from all quarters in a volume amounting to an outcry. Against some of the mothers of young children, they were extraordinarily intense and bitter; it was said that they were dirty, verminous, idle and extravagant; that they could not hold a needle and did not know the rudiments of cooking and housecraft, and that they had no control over their young children, who were untrained and animal in their habits. Some of these women were said to be foul-mouthed, bullying and abusive, given to drinking and frequenting public houses, insanitary in their habits and loose in morals.*

*These accusations were levelled against groups of women
from each and all of the evacuation areas. So obvious were their
personal shortcomings that compulsory billeting powers had to be
widely used in order to secure their accommodation in private
dwellings, and in almost every reception area there were householders who said, after a first experience, that they would defy the
law rather than takes such persons into their homes again.*

In her diary in a Norfolk village, and published in *Wartime
Women* Muriel Green wrote:

*Difficulties for the hosts were the inconvenience of having
other people in your house. Many grumbled at the dirtiness of
the evacuees, and their bad language. I have never seen such
dirty women with children. One woman who came to our shop
smelt positively filthy and her clothes were disgusting ... The
village people objected to the evacuees chiefly because of
dirtiness of their habits and clothes. Also because of their
reputed drinking and bad language. It is exceptional to hear
women swear in this village or for them to enter a public house.
The villagers used to watch them come out of the pubs with
horror.*

Most children were not with their mothers but the complaints
against these older children were even more numerous. The
Women's Group on Public Welfare explained:

*Allegations were nevertheless widespread that they were dirty
and verminous, guilty of enuresis and soiling both by day and
night, ill-clad and ill-shod, that some had never had a change
of underwear or any night clothes and had been used to sleep on
the floor, that many suffered from scabies, impetigo and other
skin diseases, that they would not eat wholesome food but
clamoured for fish and chips, sweets and biscuits, that they
would not go to bed at reasonable hours, and, finally that some
of them were destructive and defiant, foul-mouthed, liars and
pilferers.*

In Cambridge, such was the uproar against enuresis that the researcher commented that the evacuation appeared to have 'produced a Niagara all over English and Scottish country beds.'

Lucy Faithfull was sent to the Midlands as a regional welfare officer and soon found herself in the midst of a revolt. She told me:

The children from Manchester were evacuated to Derbyshire. They were really difficult and rough. I don't mean that they were unpleasant, they were enchanting, but their habits were appalling. The people of Derbyshire experienced children just doing their jobbies on the floor in the sitting rooms. The women approached the Dowager Duchess of Derbyshire who told the Ministry of Health, on behalf of the people, that they refused to have the children in their homes. I was instructed to deal with it. I was twenty-eight.

The ferocity of the complaints was soon conveyed in Parliament. Member after member rose to tell an anecdote about the dirtiness and bad behaviour of the evacuee children. Sir Henry Fildes, MP for Dumfriesshire, spoke of them as 'suffering from venereal disease, scabies and all sorts of infectious complaints.' Major Owen, MP for Caernarfonshire, considered that the 'different habits and different thoughts' of evacuees were not compatible with the kind of people who inhabited the Welsh countryside.

The accusations against the mothers are not easy to examine, to verify or disprove. No doubt, some were dirtily dressed yet there is also evidence that some were cleanly clad. What can be said is that the complaints lessened over time. In regard to the evacuee children, some figures can be cited in regard to the main grumbles, namely that they were badly clothed, were lousy, wet their beds and were ill-behaved.

Clothing. Some local authorities took note of the condition of children just before they left for evacuation. In Newcastle, 13 per cent of children were recorded as being deficient in footwear. In Manchester, 20 per cent were wearing plimsolls. Shoes were an expensive item for working-class families and their children frequently wore plimsolls

(I did). At that time Liverpool was known as 'plimsoll city'. But plimsolls were not suitable for the countryside where stout shoes were the common footwear. Not surprisingly, many foster parents (and some officials) regarded plimsolls both as deficient and also as a sign of neglect by parents.

In regard to clothing, Newcastle reckoned 21 per cent of children to be deficient and similar proportions were reported elsewhere. But what was 'deficient'? It meant that children lacked raincoats, overcoats, spare underclothes and pyjamas and other items which had been listed for the children to take with them. Clearly, then, a number of evacuees did not take the type and amount of clothing sufficient for a prolonged stay in the country. However, as will be mentioned later, poverty was widespread in urban Britain. It was not necessarily that parents did not care about their children. On the contrary, there are examples of those who made sacrifices to ensure that their children had a raincoat for the first time in their lives. It was rather that they could not afford all the recommended items. *The Cambridge Evacuation Survey* was one of the most detailed investigations of the parents of evacuees. After interviewing parents from Tottenham and Islington, the researchers concluded, in the words of Susan Issacs, 'It is hardly necessary to mention how difficult it is for the poorer London parents to provide money for clothes.'

Lice. The existence of head lice, commonly called being 'lousy', was particularly disliked by foster parents who, understandably, feared it would be passed on to their children. Further, the scratching associated with lice could open the way to impetigo, boils and eczema. In East Suffolk, the school medical officer reported that 23 per cent of evacuees were verminous, a figure in keeping with other reports. So a number—but not a majority—of evacuees were lousy. A few other reports also comment on other skin diseases. The school medical officer for Essex was cited by the Women's Group on Public Welfare as writing,

*Large numbers have been treated for impetigo, and this
condition has been very persistent in some cases, probably due*

to a poor state of health. A large number of scabies cases have also been treated at the various clinics and most have had to be removed to a special hospital for treatment.

However, it should not be deduced that lice and other skin diseases were peculiar to evacuees. Interestingly, a nationwide study of head lice infestation by Dr Kenneth Allanby was published soon after. Its findings, also used by the Women's Group On Public Welfare, revealed that infestation was wide-spread in densely populated, poverty-stricken, urban locations, but low in rural areas. Poor parents in towns were not ignorant nor unmindful about lice but they were often fighting a losing battle in over-crowded conditions, where lice were easily passed on, and in badly-lit rooms where even meticulous combing did not always allow the lice to be spotted. The more fortunate country foster parents did not always see it this way and were too ready to put the blame for lice on neglectful parents.

Bed-wetting. Figures given for the proportions of bed-wetters amongst evacuees are remarkably varied, ranging from 4 per cent to 33 per cent. The medical journal, *The Lancet*, declared:

Somewhat unexpectedly enuresis has proved to be one of the major menaces to the comfortable disposition of evacuated urban children ... every morning every window is filled with bedding hung out to air in the sunshine.

The implication behind many of the complaints was that the bed-wetting was due to bad training of the children by the parents. There were even tales of evacuee children who did not know how to use toilets. Instead, as Professor Cyril Burt, doyen of the world of psychologists, showed, enuresis was a symptom of emotional stress. In 1940 in *The British Journal of Educational Psychology* he explained that the children were being subject to the trauma of war, the emotional separation from parents, and the challenge of a new environment. Some reacted with bed-wetting. The psychologists predicted that, once the children had settled down, the bed-wetting would decrease sharply, and so it proved.

Behaviour. Figures do not appear to have been compiled on the alleged bad behaviour of evacuees. No doubt some did go scrumping, commit minor acts of delinquency and vandalism and get into fights with country children. No doubt, some were cheeky to foster parents. However, the numbers who had to be referred to child guidance clinics for persistent bad behaviour and juvenile crime were fairly low.

The conclusion, as far as a conclusion can be drawn, is that a significant minority of evacuees were ill-clad, did suffer from lice and did wet the bed. It was a minority which created severe problems for their foster parents. However, these difficulties of a minority gave vent to exaggerated tales which were then used to condemn the majority. Further, the poor clothing and lice infestation were more a reflection of poverty than neglect, while the bed-wetting was a symptom of stress, not bad training. Meanwhile, how did Lucy Faithfull get on with the revolt in Derbyshire? She explained:

> *The town clerk of Derby made the town hall available and notices were sent out. The Duchess mustered all her friends from the county houses, the billeting officers got the foster parents and the town hall was full. The Duchess was in the chair and said, 'Miss Faithfull, we want the Government to know that we think these children should be kept in camps and not in private houses where they disrupt lives and damage furniture with their habits.' Several people spoke from the floor and platform and finally I was expected to speak. I said that I appreciated their difficulties but that war was hard. I went on, 'I want to ask you one question: if we put all the children under canvas or in a hall or all together elsewhere and it was bombed and all the children were killed, would you really feel happy?' There was a silence and finally one woman got up and said, 'I can't possibly face such a situation. I'll take children.' From that moment we had no trouble.*

In time the Derbyshire foster parents and evacuee children adapted to each other. Similar adaptations occurred elsewhere and the complaints began to lessen.

The ferocity of the early criticisms of the evacuees may have been fuelled by the foster parents' resentments against the way the system was working, for they had two major grievances against the organization of the evacuation scheme. One was that, although billeting was supposed to be compulsory, the richer sections of the community were able to escape. Exemption could be won via a medical certificate saying the householder was unfit to take evacuees. Reports from billeting officers and comments from neutral observers like teachers, indicate that the system was abused on behalf of rich and powerful members of the community. One billeting officer told Richard Titmuss that he could wallpaper his office with their certificates. In one country town, prominent citizens did not take evacuees. These included the vicar, the town clerk, the bank manager and the chief billeting officer himself. One MP gained exemption on the grounds that he often left confidential papers about his large house. Some middle-class foster parents thus found themselves resenting the privileges of the rich while condemning the vices of the poor. The British class system was brought into sharp focus by evacuation.

The other complaint about the system concerned the level of payments to foster parents. They received ten shillings and sixpence for the first child and eight shillings and sixpence for subsequent children. Following much agitation, periodic increases did follow but only by small amounts. The allowances were supposed to cover board and lodging with the children's own parents providing clothing. But many foster parents had higher standards of living than the natural parents and thus found themselves clothing the children at their own expense. Further, food prices rose by 14 per cent within a few months, and the allowances were never raised accordingly. As taking foster children was compulsory, the feeling prevailed that the subsidy foster parents made to looking after evacuees was an enforced tax not imposed upon the rest of the community. Many of the foster parents' grumbles were eventually smoothed out, but the complaints about allowances proved a running sore which lasted the length of the evacuation.

It might seem that all foster parents regretted their experiences with the evacuees. This impression arises from the enormous publicity, in press and Parliament, given to the early days of evacuation in 1939 when complaints were at their height. But the impression tells only part of the story for, even at the start, there were foster parents who wholeheartedly welcomed, helped and enjoyed the evacuees. As one middle-class foster mother—or hostess as she chose to be called—put it in those early months, quoted in *Borrowed Children*,

> *Though most of the hostesses in the village seem contented with their foster children, I am, of course, speaking only for myself when I say that my six boys are making this dreary, lonely war not only tolerable, but often enjoyable.*

The effort, sacrifice and sense of reward is even more vividly portrayed in *War Wives* by a woman who took two evacuees and explained,

> *There was an accommodation allowance made but it didn't even cover their food, let alone clothes. However, the next morning (Saturday) we got a friend to come and stay with them while we went into Wellington, the nearest market town. We had to buy them everything—complete sets of underwear, dresses, coats, macs, socks and shoes. Most people in Coalbrookdale and Iron Bridge who had taken in evacuees found themselves in the same predicament. They also had to rush out and get clothes for the majority of these children. The tradespeople in Wellington were wonderful and knocked quite a percentage off the total expenditure for us. They decided that was a way in which they could help.*
>
> *We got our little girls a beautiful coat and hat set each— lovely quality. Later I would have loved to have been able to afford coats like those for my own children, but rationing made it impossible. They were thrilled to try on everything when we returned. They really did look better after a good night's sleep and dressed in clothes that fitted.*

We decided that they should call us Auntie and Uncle and to this they readily agreed. In the next day or two we had a visit from the clinic people to help advise with any problems that may have arisen, and to point out those that would. The inherent problem that most of us found out to our cost was bed-wetting on a problem scale! And verminous heads which had to be tackled daily, night and morning, combing with a fine-tooth comb over a large piece of paper, applying a special pomade and washing regularly with clinical soap. It really was quite a chore, but to them it became almost a game. They would regularly vie with each other to see who had the most lice and would become quite excited over the grand total. They would greet my husband when he returned in the evening with, 'Uncle, I had 138 today and Winnie only had 120!'

It ceased to be funny when my husband, at a conference with his Chief and several other GECB executives, in response to a tickle on his cheek, brushed off one of the aforesaid offenders onto his notes—much to his chagrin! So he too had to line up with them night and morning to have the 'livestock' removed with the fine-tooth comb.

The bed-wetting proved a much greater problem in many homes—very difficult to eradicate and the endless washing incurred was heartbreaking. There were no machines in those days—it all had to be done the hard way, by hand. To say nothing of the endless ironing and drying. The clinic advised there should be punishment when the bed was wet and praise when it was dry. They suggested keeping something that they really enjoyed from them when they had fallen from grace and restoring it on 'good' days.

They had never used cutlery before for eating, only a spoon when necessary. With us they had their own knife, fork and spoon with which they were thrilled. On days when there was not a good report, just a spoon was set out for the guilty one, while the other had the full set of cutlery. This they soon learned to accept without a word—and it worked wonders. Gradually it became perhaps twice a week and then they would be dry for a week or two, and eventually scarcely a lapse—and finally DRY!

My life had become very different from what I had imagined as a new housewife. I had acquired a ready-made family of four, so our life together as husband and wife was severely curtailed. Our social life was practically non-existent. On the other hand, it was quite amazing to see how those children blossomed physically. It was most heartening and gratifying to see them develop into two plump, healthy, well-behaved, really very nice little girls. We both found it very rewarding.

This account probably reflects the dedication of many foster parents. Certainly, the second and third phases of the evacuation proceeded without the uproar of the first one. As far as the foster parents were concerned, the evacuation grew more positive with time. Some reasons are as follows:

The right foster parents. After a few months, the most glaring mismatches between foster parents and children were sorted out. Some, not all, of the most unsuitable foster parents were weeded out.

Support. The welfare authorities began to offer support to the foster parents.

The children began to settle down. The 'Niagara' deluge of urine slowed down. Even the lice scare subsided. In the second and third evacuations, the sending authorities introduced medical examinations and treatment before children departed. Often the treatment was no more than the dreaded 'hair raid' and shampoo but it was successful. Thus, in June 1940, of 670 children sent from Shepherd's Bush, only two were infested on arrival while of well over a thousand children from Manchester, the number was eighty. After the initial shock at the condition of the first evacuees, foster parents even began to identify with them and to take their side. In 1940, a report was issued on evacuation in Wantage (a village where I was staying). Commenting on this report, Mrs St Loe Strachey noted that foster parents were now talking about their evacuees as 'a very nice lot' while still referring to those in other villages as 'impossible, dirty, naughty children.' The latter, she drily added, were, like ghosts, only seen by other people. The report itself concluded that the placements were now proceeding well but recommended that 'the experience of the first days of evacuation ... must never be repeated.'

The 'phoney war' ended and the real Blitz began. This was perhaps the most important reason. Once the bombs descended in 1940, the foster parents knew that they were giving essential protection to children. The second and third evacuations often conveyed the same children who were in the first one, but the sufferings from which they fled provoked sympathy, not resentment, in those who cared for them.

For many foster parents, especially for those who kept the children for some years, the evacuation experience was worthwhile and fulfilling. The depth of the relationships forged in some homes is evidenced in the pain both adults and children felt when they did part and in the fact that many maintained contact after the war. Some older foster parents stated that the evacuees gave them a second family and brought new meaning to their lives. Some evacuees remained forever grateful to the protection, guidance and love they received. Richard Titmuss rightly pays a rich tribute to the foster parents. He speaks of a

willingness on the part of householders in the reception areas to accept responsibilities and make sacrifices in the national interest. It is not easy to generalize about the manner in which these responsibilities were discharged, and it is impossible to discuss in detail all that was involved in caring for other people's children. No records were kept of householders and evacuees who met each other in a spirit of tolerance and overcame the difficulties of living together. No facts remain to measure the patience extended to unruly, spoilt, neglected, noisy and dirty children. Domestic successes were not talked about, publicised or reported; the misfits and the disharmonies were. Occasionally and by exception there came into the official records examples of householders who in the later war years were still caring for the children they had received in 1939. But the great majority of householders who co-operated with the authorities could not help regarding the reception of evacuees as an invasion of fundamental rights, an interference with their comings and goings, a violation of the intimacies and ease of domestic life. For the authorities to impose—and to maintain for almost five years—a policy of billeting in private homes was a severe test of the better side of human nature. It was a formidable—to some an intolerable—burden for any Government to place on a section of its people. A community less kindly, less self-controlled, less essentially Christian in behaviour, would not have acquiesced to the same extent and for such a long period of time as this one did.

The mothers

Of all the participants in the evacuation, it was probably the mothers of evacuated children who had the most difficult time. Lucy Faithfull pointed out to me that little consideration has been given to the feelings of mothers (or fathers) who sent their children away, probably feeling that their choice was between exposing their children to danger at home or being parted from those they loved. She said:

We should also remember the suffering of the parents who stayed at home while the children were evacuated. In those days, working-class people didn't travel so to be parted was the more terrible. They had to let their children go into the unknown, they had no choice about where they went.

Mothers with young children could accompany them and hence many thousands of young women also became evacuees. Probably they had the hardest time of all those who did go away. They were placed in billets where the householder was paid five shillings per adult and three shillings per child for mothers and accompanied children. However, this amount was for lodgings only and the mothers had to buy and cook their own food. Once they had queued to obtain the food with their ration coupons—and prices were rising while coupons were in short supply—the mothers had then to prepare and cook meals in somebody else's kitchen. This sharing of kitchens appeared to lead to frequent disagreements with the mothers feeling they were being criticized by the house-holders for their lack of domestic skills.

The response of many evacuee mothers was to spend as much time as possible out of the house. So they and their small children trailed around small towns and villages, often in cold weather, looking for somewhere to eat. Unfortunately, the lack of cafes and social centres served to intensify their sense of isolation and unhappiness. In *Wartime Women* we read of the mothers' plight, from Muriel Green's wartime diary:

Food was much dearer at the village grocer's. Nothing can be bought ready-cooked and they did not understand the coal cooking ranges of the country. They all grumbled at the inconveniences of travel, now only one bus each way every two hours and about three times a day. They were not used to living three miles from a station and a bus station. Some said there was no cinema and one wanted to know where she could get her hair permed. They found the country very quiet and lacked amusement. One woman said, 'I'd rather be bombed on me own door-step than stay here and die of depression.'

If the mothers did escape to cinemas, they might be criticized for wasting money and if they went to pubs, accused of flirting with the local men.

The difficulties and dilemmas of young mothers were well explained by one who had twice given birth during air raids. She did not want to be parted from her husband, who worked in the docks, but, after their house was bombed, she agreed to go. She wrote, recorded in *War Wives*:

When we got to Staffordshire we were put in a hall, to find people who would let us stay in their home, for the time being. We had some food and drink, but, sad to say, my daughters and

I were the only ones that no one seemed to want. A couple with a young daughter were told to take us and we went to their house. The room we were put in, the rain came in, and a couple of pails were left in the room to collect the rainwater.

After we were there a while, my elder daughter was put in a school. I had to take my younger daughter out of the house during the day because the woman's little daughter used to pinch and claw my little girl whenever she saw her. After a few weeks in Stafford, I asked my husband if it would be all right to come back. He said, 'Yes, we'll be all together.' So we came back and we all slept together on the floor, and if we had an explosion, or if my husband was fire-watching, we slept in the shelter at the top of the road.'

Given stories like these, it was no surprise that the Report by the Commission of the Churches should conclude:

The town mothers themselves were almost invariably unhappy in the country ... There was also financial difficulty for the mothers connected with the upkeep of two households, and clothing for country wear was an added expense.

Lonely, in an unfamiliar environment, facing financial difficulties, missing relatives, it was the evacuee mothers who led the returns back to the danger zones. But it was not all gloom. Some mothers did feel at home with their hosts and made long-term friendships. One example is cited by Ruth Inglis in *The Children's War* of a mother who wrote the following:

I was living in Lambeth in the late 30s and became part of the September 1st scheduled evacuation. My son and I were billeted at a lovely village pub called 'The King's Arms' in the village of Langton Matravers in Dorset. It was so entirely different to see rolling green hills, cows and sheep, instead of the grim bricks and mortar that was Lambeth. My son was five years old and I was twenty-six. They were very kind and loving towards us. My son adjusted to it—he went to a good school there—and I

*straight away thought it was like paradise, especially after what
we had left behind. My son and I were never homesick and never
wanted to go back to London. We were too happy enjoying the
beautiful scenery. It has given us an enduring love of Dorset. To
cap everything, I had a wonderful job as a laboratory assistant
at the Technical Research Establishment there.*

*We were away almost six years but we had to come back to
London as my home was there and all my belongings. We
returned the year war ended under duress from my family. I was
not shocked by the bomb damage as I had lived among it from
time to time when visiting my parents. But I never did feel cut
off from my family as Dorset was the love of my son's life and
mine. I look back at my time there as one full of happiness and
love—in fact, as far as I'm concerned, Langton Matravers is
'Paradise Lost'.*

Perhaps that mother was unusual in being happily settled from
the start to the end of the war. What is certain is that more young
mothers started to settle once the authorities began to provide
services for them (of which more in the next chapter) and following
the introduction of the assisted evacuation scheme.

One of the great failings of the original scheme was that it rendered
the accompanying mothers powerless. They had no choice over their
destination and no choice over their billet. The assisted scheme
allowed mothers to choose both. Despite a great shortage of accommodation, many did succeed in finding rooms where they could be in
sole charge of and could cook for their children. For them, evacuation
then became a much more satisfying experience.

The children

Lucy Faithfull was involved in the evacuation from beginning to
end. Looking back at it after fifty years, she was quite sure that it
would have been better if the evacuation could have been avoided.
But the fact was that it could not have been avoided, so the
question still arises, what did evacuation mean to the children
concerned?

Any children separated from their families and homes are likely to suffer some unhappiness and distress. These normal reactions were heightened for the evacuee children by factors associated with the war. For a start they had the insecurity of initially not knowing where they were going and, once there, of not knowing when they would return home. Then there were anxieties about the safety of their parents. All the older children knew that their mothers were in districts subject to bombing. Some also had fathers fighting abroad. Mrs St Loe Strachey records that foster mothers tried not to talk about the war in front of the children:

But on two occasions the children came back from school having heard in the village, 'Bombers over England' and at dinner asked anxiously 'Did they get to . . .?' (the large port in the North-West from which they came).

Sadly, at times, their fears were realized and children had to return home for funerals or have the news broken to them that a father had been killed in action.

The problems associated with separation, however, could be eased by a number of factors. First, and perhaps most important, were the attitudes of the foster parents. Later, in a war-time broadcast, the psychiatrist, Donald Winnicott emphasized the important contribution of understanding foster parents who were able to accept the children's distress while constantly providing affection and security. Second in importance were the efforts of the school teachers who accompanied the school parties. In reading contemporary accounts, it becomes clear that many teachers accepted responsibilities far beyond their teaching duties. Leah Manning was a former teacher and MP who was employed by the Government to inspect reception areas. In her autobiography, *A Life for Education* she wrote:

Not enough praise has ever been given to my colleagues who accompanied the children. From comfortable flats and homes they often found themselves in the most primitive conditions. 'The loo in my cottage is at the bottom of a long garden,' complained one elderly lady. 'It's always raining. You don your gum boots, mackintosh, take your umbrella.' Poor old dear, but every evening she set out with her wet weather paraphernalia to visit any child who had been absent from school, in case anything was wrong. Others so enjoyed the little country schools, the possibility of experiment, that when evacuation ended they opted to stay in their country schools.

Many teachers took a personal interest in every evacuated child in their class. They visited them in their foster homes and organized out-of-school activities. In addition, they represented the children's home territory and were a visible link with home. The full story of the contribution of the teachers has still to be written.

Third, local residents in the reception areas often took it upon themselves to ease the lot of the incomers. The publicity given to some local hostility to evacuees in 1939 has detracted from the efforts of those who welcomed them. In *William and the Evacuees*, Richmal Crompton laughingly portrays The Committee of Residents for the Entertainment of Evacuees, including William's mother, sitting around the vicarage table and, having supplied clothes, food and parties, puzzle over what else they can do for the evacuee children. One mother sighs:

'When one thinks of one's own dear children safe and happy at home one feels that one must do something to brighten the lives of these little waifs.'

'They're not waifs exactly,' objected Mrs Monks.

'Waifs to all intents and purposes,' said Mrs Poppleham firmly. 'Taken from their homes, bereft of a parent's care.'

Having dealt with their evacuees, the committee decided to offer a party to those in the next village—much to the chagrin of William and the Outlaws who considered they deserved a party.

Fortunately, most villagers did not look upon the evacuees as waifs but many did rally round to supply material and emotional support to the newcomers.

Fourth, the evacuees were helped when efforts were made to maintain contact between them and their home areas. Here the churches played an important role. In East London, Father Groser organized visits by the clergy to evacuees in Brighton and Eastbourne where they both took news from home and also facilitated contacts between them and local churches. Other home churches printed newsletters which were sent to those who had gone from their parishes and ensured that all the children received a present at Christmas. Some churches even organized periodic exchanges of clergy so that the latest news from both ends could be circulated.

Even more significant was contact with parents. Difficulties of finance and travel did restrict visiting while, as mentioned, the visits could prove awkward for foster parents and parents. Yet, as Boyd observed in *Evacuation in Scotland*, children who did receive visits acquired a sense 'of continuing interest... necessary for a happy settlement.'

To sum up: there were factors working for and against the placements. It is not surprising, therefore, that children had a great variety of experiences. Some children were unhappy. They could be unhappy if parents failed to visit. Ben Wicks records the sadness of one girl in *No Time To Wave Goodbye*. She wrote:

> *We used to go to the coaches on a Sunday to see if our mother got off the coach and when she wasn't there we used to walk home sadly. The postman became an obsession for me. I used to see him and want to rush up to him and ask if there were any letters.*

They could be unhappy because they disliked their foster parents (or the foster parents disliked them). Sometimes children had to be moved for these and other reasons leading to much instability. When I interviewed Eric Buchanan he told me that he did not settle in his first foster home in Chew Magna and was moved to another which he liked: but then his mother came to take him home to London. When the bombs did descend on London he was sent to Windsor until, after another lull, he was called back home. More bombs fell, so it was back to Windsor until that town became a target, so it was back to London again. Soon after, the flying bombs started, and so, this time with his mother, he went to relatives in Aberdeen. That did not work out so they moved on to Torrey. Moves occurred for many reasons but, whatever the reasons, they were unsettling and made it more difficult for the children to settle in schools and neighbourhoods and to make friends.

Evacuees could be unhappy if not accepted by local children. Sometimes the latter were jealous of evacuees. William of *Just William* fame was once confronted by a deputation of his friends who moaned:

> 'They get all the fun.'
> 'Yes,' grumbled Frankie Miller, a small, stout, snub-nosed boy of seven. 'They got a Christmas party an' a Christmas tree.'

William responded by 'vacuating' his friends and organizing a party for them. More seriously, resentment could occur because local children saw the evacuees as responsible for over-crowding at schools and in homes. They could sneer at the newcomers as 'skinnies' (because they were so much thinner than country children) or 'vaccies' as we were called in Hastings. Sometimes fights occurred between the two groups.

Laurie Laken, from the Isle of Dogs in London, is an example of someone who was unhappily evacuated. We have been life-long friends since our teens. We were both evacuated yet it is only in recent years that we have shared our experiences. Laurie and his brothers had short evacuations but then returned to Goodmayes. Once the doodle-bugs came, they were sent away for a longer period. He told me:

> We all met in the school and went by train to Macclesfield. This time Mum didn't come with us. There was the waving goodbye and the fear that we would not see them again. We had no idea where we were going, we just got on the train. We were three brothers and mum had asked the billeting officer to keep us

91

together. When we got to Macclesfield, we were taken to a big hall, all lined up, and people came in, pointed at you and picked you out. We were three and nobody wanted us. So the hall emptied and we were left. But later a truck came and a man took us. He had six kids of his own. It was a terrible place. They put us in a small room high in the building. The three of us had to sleep on two canvas camp beds so we took it in turns to sleep in the middle which was the most uncomfortable place. We never related to the couple. She was a big woman. He was a dirty, old man, he used to spit in the fire. He never abused us but he shouted and we kept out of his way. A neighbour, a young mother, used to keep an eye on us. She took us to see Snow White and the Seven Dwarfs. I related more with her as a mother figure.

We used to write home. Mum came to visit us and was appalled at the conditions. We all got lice, fleas. I remember being in school and brushing my hand through my hair and all kinds of live things dropped out. We went to the barbers one day for a normal hair cut and he just whipped it all off and we came out literally bald. That was a great stigma and I can remember standing outside the shop picking the fleas out of my brother's head. We were called names by other kids because it was thought dirty. It was more upsetting because there was no-one we could talk to about it.

I remember liking oatcake for breakfast and big chunks of bread and cheese. For dinner we were given a pudding basin and told to get chips and then eat them outside in the cold. We were hungry. I can remember following a man who was eating an apple and waiting for him to throw the core away so that I could pick it up and eat it.

When Mum came up she told us about the things she was sending us in parcels. 'Did you get the chocolate and the walnuts?' We said not but that we had seen walnut shells in the dustbin. So they were opening our parcels. Mum slept in the house that night and when she went down she saw the cockroaches. She must then have spoken to the billeting officer. We all got moved.

My older brother, Ken, then went to a nice family. He had passed the scholarship at home and now he went to the grammar school. Roy and I were put into a hostel for evacuees. There were about a dozen of us there. I had a fight the first night because somebody pinched Roy's comic. It was a big detached house in grounds, run by two ladies, a matron and an assistant matron.

We slept in dormitories, very austere. We used to have to go to bed and not talk. I remember always praying every night, 'Keep Mum safe tonight.' We got punished if we talked and I remember having to bend over the bed and getting the slipper.

Roy got diphtheria. He was put up in the attic in isolation. That was sad for I knew people died from it. I couldn't go up to see him so I used to shout up the spiral staircase to see if he was all right. Then he was taken to hospital. The whole hostel had to be isolated and I remember all lining up and having our throats swabbed by the doctor. He recovered.

I can remember Mum coming to visit and taking us over to a park to feed the ducks. I was wishing she would take us back but she said that things were so bad at home that she couldn't.

A lady used to come into the hostel and take activities. She was a surrogate mother figure really. I was very fond of her and I used to be up at the window waiting for her. Painting and colouring, making things, ludo and games at the table. We didn't go out anywhere.

The food was good. We used to sing as a group with the matron. The words were, Way down Highfield House, far, far, away; Where we get bread and cheese three times a day; Eggs and bacon we don't see; We get sawdust in our tea; That's why we're gradually fading away.

There was a garden and we could climb the trees and swing on the ropes. And a sandpit. It was regimented and controlled. I had a puppet which I'd made at school back home. It fitted on my hand and I used to talk to it a lot and got comfort from that. I look back on it as a rotten experience. It did make me appreciate home more and I was glad to get home after the war.

There were other unhappy children like Laurie Laken. Perhaps worse were those who were exploited and abused. Children fostered on farms, and occasionally in shops, could be used as cheap labour. In the many letters and accounts compiled by Ben Wicks, some instances of sexual abuse have come to light. Usually, these accounts, looking back at evacuation after many years, were the first time the abused were able to articulate what happened to them.

One woman revealed, that, as a five-year-old, she had been stripped and abused a number of times by the two teenage sons of her foster parents. Others were touched by foster fathers. It is impossible to say how widespread was such abuse. It is definite that the victims suffered much physical and emotional harm. As the former five-year-old later wrote, 'I can never forgive what they did to me, and it has affected me all my life.'

As well as the accounts of unhappy children, there are other, probably more, accounts from those who enjoyed evacuation and regarded it as a happy and positive experience. One such was Anne Buchanan, now the wife of Eric. She told me:

War was declared one day, the next day we were told to get ready for evacuation, the next day my dad joined the army. We then left from Govan (in Glasgow); there was my mother, my older sister aged nine, me aged seven, a sister of five, one of three, and then the only boy, baby Ross, just ten weeks. We went to Galston in Ayrshire. It was on a farm and we had just one room and the use of a toilet. My mum had to cope on a £4 allowance from my dad. We got parish clothes, after a means test. We got school clothes, gym slips, jumpers, stockings and shoes. Some children used to kid us a bit about parish clothes but a lot had them. We could wander around the farm and were allowed to keep any eggs we found on the ground. The farmer's wife also gave us scones so we did well. The billeting officer was good to us and used to bring us stuff at Christmas. We didn't have toys but we made our own fun. Coming from the town to the country, it was a life on its own. It was very nice.

After about a year, we got moved to a little cottage—it must have been nearby because we still went to the same school. It was a little house on its own but there was no furniture in it until the billeting officer got us some stuff. There was one bed and we all slept in it. No electricity, paraffin lamps. And people were kind. Sometimes we used to find a couple of rabbits hanging on the door. We never knew who left them. We'd hardly ever seen a rabbit and the first time we didn't know how to cook it. The billeting officer showed us how to skin it. We all got involved doing it and afterwards we loved rabbit stew. One night we were all in bed in the dark. Our mother used to sing to us and get us all singing. But this night we heard a knocking on the door and we were too scared to answer it. Finally the person shouted out. It was our dad, home on leave. We used to have to walk to school, five miles. But we joined up with the village children and found short cuts across the fields.

We moved on to a gatehouse on an estate. There was another evacuated family there already and the woman was terrible. Food was rationed and her children got the best. Some soldiers were stationed on the estate and they used to give us rations, stew and iron biscuits. A knitting bee was started in the big house with the woman of the house, four or five land army girls, and my mother who would take my sister and me in turns. My sister was a good knitter, I wasn't. We were sharing the knitting of an RAF scarf. Her part would be all neat and then my bit all bulging out and so on.

Our next place was near Girvan where we got our own little terraced house. But there was no water and we had to use a pump in the street. The toilet was in the garden and at night we all used to go down together with a candle. The village people had put furniture in to help us. We joined the Sunday school and went to church. If there was a dance in the town hall we all went together as a family. We stayed there quite a while. Our mum became like a friend to us, a pal, she went everywhere with us. Once a week she took my older sister and me to the pictures as a treat because we helped with the little ones. We all mucked in together. I left school at fourteen and started work in

*a hotel. Then Dad came home. He had been captured at
Dunkirk and in a prisoner of war camp. So we stayed for the
whole war although others went back early. We got on with
other people. We had a great time.*

John Whitwell, now a vicar in East London, was three when the
war broke out. Having endured the Blitz in Dagenham, his docker
father and his mother decided that the doodle-bugs were too
dangerous and put him on the official evacuation. John told me:

*I remember going down to the station, Becontree, not knowing
where we were going and we finished up in Morecambe. I well
remember standing in rows in a church hall and the ladies
picking us out one by one. It seemed to me that we were like
slaves at an auction market.*

*But I fell on my feet because my evacuee landlady was the
wife of the owner of the laundry so they were fairly well-off,
middle-class people. They had an eighteen-year-old son who
was at college and so I could play with his old toys. This was
1944–45, an eight-year-old boy from East London who enjoyed
a year at the seaside.*

*I was homesick for the first few days. It was the first time
I had been away from both Mum and Dad. Mrs Lamb, the
foster mother, was very good. We didn't have phones and she
encouraged me to write home once a week. In return, Mum
used to send food parcels. Then I made friends, went to
school and settled down. I was the only child in the foster
home and I reckon I was spoilt. It was a nice, middle-class
home, very different from our home in Dagenham. I
remember having Yorkshire pudding before the main meal.
They were from Yorkshire. She was a good cook, made
marvellous lemon meringue pies. And I remember seeing the
Lake District across Morecambe Bay and I've always liked
the Lakes since then.*

*I went to the Saturday morning cinema club. We didn't
have TV then so films were a tremendous treat. I remember the
George Formby films and seeing the news, it was all about*

winning the war. There were special meetings for evacuees, a
Christmas party.

My parents could not visit so when Mum appeared in May
1945, it seemed rather strange to me. I almost didn't know her
and had to adjust again to having another mother figure.

Evacuation was an opportunity to see the wider world, the
Dagenham equivalent of going to boarding school. It was a
positive experience. Evacuation enabled young people from
urban areas to see a world they would not have seen, to live with
people from different backgrounds and different walks of life. It
broke down barriers and gave us an assurance we would not have
had. It made one a bit more independent, a bit more self-assured.

While at Morecambe, I was sent to Sunday School and
when I got back to London I continued it. I then went to cubs,
scouts, the church choir. I hadn't done that before. Back in
Dagenham I went to Monteagle Junior School, the same as
George Carey, now Archbishop of Canterbury, and then to
Dagenham County High School. I think evacuation made me
think I could do anything I wanted to. I even set my sights on
going into the Foreign Office. It was only later that I realized
that this was not expected for Dagenham people.

If John Whitwell considered that evacuation took him into a
different culture, Morecambe rather than Dagenham, how much
more so for the evacuees who lived at Dartington Hall. Their
teacher, Margaret Stevens, quoted in *Evacuees at Dartington*
enthused over the advantages of residing at this progressive and
private school. She described how the school's co-founder,
Dorothy Elmhirst, used to invite the pupils

to evening coffee where we met such people as Margot Fonteyn
and Robert Helpmann in their early careers.

Imogen Holst was another welder of the evacuees into the
community, organising the first children's Christmas Carol
Concert in the Great Hall, bringing together through music the
children from Dartington Hall School, the Village School and
ourselves. Her students were often to be found working with our

children. Other notable people who brought their special talents
and experience to our community included Jenny Gertz who, on
returning from internment and although convalescing,
introduced Laban Movement to some of the staff and worked
with the children in the Open Air Theatre; Winsome Bartlett
who introduced country dancing with her pipe and tabor and
George Bennett who entertained us with films.

Some of the boys who began to show an interest in
agriculture were given opportunities to assist on local farms at
weekends and in the holidays. These and other extra curricular
opportunities gave unique experiences to the children and despite
very little equipment they were given a wider education than
most war time evacuees received.

If tears were the measurement of what degree of happiness
and security had meant to the children in five years of
evacuation, then the amount was immeasurable on the day of
departure. Of the extent of the quality of life they had been
given no one will ever know, except by realising the tremendous
depth of influence Dartington gave to us, the then young
teachers. Perhaps the fact that there are today a few men and
women living and working in and around Dartington and
Totnes who were once those evacuees is an indication of what
those halcyon days in the midst of a terrible war gave.
Dartington was to leave its indelible mark upon all of us.

Few children could benefit from Dartington. But many could
and did enjoy the countryside. A frequent theme found in
accounts of evacuation is the surprise and delight evacuee children discovered in rural areas. Lucy Faithfull explained that many
evacuee children had never before left what were called 'the
slums'. Soon after one group arrived, she took them for a walk
across the fields where they encountered some cows. One child
exclaimed, 'Miss, whatever are those, horses with handlebars?'

A young teacher, evacuated with her class from Walthamstow,
soon perceived that the small children in her care could gain much
from the country. She wrote in her diary (and quoted in *Wartime*
Women):

*We gathered the children together at least once a day and took
them for walks. They just revelled in the glorious sunshine—
what a Godsend it was during those difficult days. Since that
first week we have taken the children out for rambles in the
country and their knowledge of Nature is unlimited. All the
nature lessons we had endeavoured to take in the classroom had
suddenly become real. The kiddies are fascinated by all the
beauty of nature and their keen observation and interest
astonishes us daily. Never before have they had the
opportunities that this life has given them of admiring the
beauty and wonder of God's Handiwork.*

*After the first month when we had no school assemblies
we were able to share a school with the local people and have
had alternate weeks on morning and afternoon shifts. When
we are not in school pegging away at the 3 Rs, we become the
Evacuee Hikers. This exercise in the beautiful fresh air has
made a difference to the health and well-being of these
children.*

Of course, the children above were not speaking for themselves.
But other, older, children did. Eric Buchanan, after moving to a
second foster home, delighted in the country life. He told me:

*It was marvellous. A smallholding outside the village. Again I
was the only child. The foster father had a big three-wheel bike
which he rode to his work. He was a miner and had a bath every
time he came back. My bedroom was in the loft next to the place
where the apples were stored. I got sick of apples. They had a pig
and chickens. I used to clean out the pig sty every day and they
paid me a halfpenny a week. A city boy to a smallholding on his
own, it was a wonderful experience.*

*Being on my own, I used to wander around and explore the
countryside. I remember on a summer's day, lying in a field and
looking up at the blue sky and watching skylarks. And all
around were yellow summer flowers. It was my first taste of the
beauty of the countryside. I remember seeing a water-mill where
they made cider.*

That experience instilled into Eric Buchanan a love for the countryside which never left him. After years as a busy Salvation Army officer on urban council estates, he has recently retired—to a small village in the country.

Leslie Thomas is now a world famous author. As a boy he spent some years in the care of Dr Barnardo's. He was in a residential establishment called Goldings when it was evacuated to the country. For him, it was a turning point, as he relates in his autobiography, *This Time Next Week*:

Somewhere along the way, I suppose, there comes to everyone a time when they realise and mark the things that to them are beautiful and good. This is not necessarily a gradual thing. It can take all your life, it is true, or it can take a few weeks or months.

With me it took only a late summer, an autumn and part of a winter. In that time, when I was thirteen, I discovered the things, or the beginnings of them, that I have always loved. I did not stop caring about the other things. I still played football and had fights and threw stones but I had a new awareness of things.

We had left Goldings after a month and gone to Narborough, a village in Norfolk. About half the boys from Kingston were already there in an obese and elderly house just outside the village, on the road to King's Lynn.

It was here that I came to know the things I loved.

Afternoons in winter when the light goes early; water in its wild state, and shadows on water; lanes and roads in summer, empty and dusty; voices calling across fields at night. And strong, sweet tea, and warm jerseys; wild animals who do not see you first; trees, any sort; old maps and books and letters, brown and full of secret things. Every clear morning; simple, beautiful words. Seagulls, big blackbirds and homecomings ...

The first weeks there were full of hot days; days, it seems now of an almost mythical boyhood summer. Clean high mornings over the trees, big skies, sun all the time until we were tired, and then the misty evenings.

The same children could have both happy and unhappy experiences. This is well illustrated in an account by an eleven-year-old girl in Audrey Jones' book *Farewell Manchester* in which she gives her own account of the Manchester evacuation:

We settled down in our new home. They were very nice people but we lived for Saturday when my mother came to see us and told us that Dad could not come as he had been made an ARP Warden for the district; but he sent his love and would visit soon. She said the house was very quiet with us all gone. After a while we had to move to another family as the lady we were with was going to have another baby and was not well. So we moved in with a large family with three grown up sons and a daughter, who made a fuss of us and we were soon one of the family.

My brother in the meantime had settled in on the farm helping with jobs, bringing in cows to milk, etc. They had a grown up son who had to go in the forces. Mum and Dad used to come on Saturday and bring a picnic with them and we would have it in a field on the farm. I used to go once a week with the lady we were staying with to the cinema. I think she could only afford to take one of us, but my sister was happy playing on the farm. One day I got a letter from my mother to say we were going home. We could not wait for Saturday to come. The first thing I saw on my arrival home was the huge balloons in the sky; they looked like great big airships. Then one night we had an air raid. We lived in the industrial part of Manchester and it was very frightening, so mother decided we must go back. Once again we went to Bollington.

This time we were placed with a young couple and a baby and I am sorry to say it was to be a bad experience for us. The first night we were there the sirens went but the man said it was alright for us to go to bed as they only passed over going to the cities. The room we slept in was bare except for two camp beds with one blanket on each. By now it was winter; we lay there cold and frightened as the planes went over. I brought my sister onto my camp bed and we shared the two blankets, wondering if we could find our way home along the tram lines. The food was also poor and when we came home from school there was never anyone in. When we did get a meal it was only a jam butty (as they called it then). I could see my sister was not well; she was not very strong as a child and a poor eater. I wrote to my mum and told her. She came straight away and took us to the Billeting Officer in charge of finding accommodation. He was very upset that we had not been properly looked after. My mum told him that although we were a poor family, we were used to a good bed and food and she was taking us home. By this time my brother had settled in with his new family, a policeman and his wife and children. The Officer told my mother that he had a good place for us, so we made our way once again to a new family.

It was a lovely house. They were a middle aged couple with a daughter—and what a spread she made, and what a contrast to our last home! I remember the first night we were bathed, fed and given a dressing gown each, as we didn't possess one in those days, and we went to bed happy. We soon made friends with their daughter. She was shy at first, being an only child. The lady taught us to knit scarves, gloves etc and used to take us to Macclesfield shopping. I remember on one shopping trip she told me I would have to have my hair cut short. I had long wavy hair, my dad's pride and joy. Imagine when he came to see us—he was very annoyed that she had taken it on herself to cut it without permission. However, my mum said it was alright and easier for the lady to keep clean. So peace reigned.

One Saturday morning we woke to find there had been a heavy snowfall. Our first thought was to get to the station to meet my mum, as she would find it hard getting up the hill in that weather, but our substitute parents told us we couldn't go out in the snow drifts and that our mum would find her way alright. We waited by the window and had given her up when she appeared with my brother. He had gone to the station to

meet her and help her up the hill; my dad was working
weekends by then. My mother's health was not so good by now
and after talking it over with my dad they decided to bring us
home as they were missing us so much. The family were upset
that we were going home as their daughter had got really
friendly with us by this time and would miss us, but my mother
and father decided to have us home.

We went through some scarey times in the air raids but
thank God we all came through it safe together. My brother
kept in touch with his host family; they all attended his
wedding and he still goes to see the lady (sadly, the husband
died).

The many personal accounts of evacuation suggest that children
responded in a great variety of ways. Has research anything to add?
The major investigation of evacuees occurred at Cambridge under
the leadership of Susan Issacs—*The Cambridge Evacuation
Survey*—concentrated on 373 children evacuated from Tottenham and 352 from Islington. The researchers examined files, had
the children write essays about their evacuation experiences and
talked to some foster parents and natural parents. In regard to
assessing the success of placements they asked welfare visitors and
teachers to make a judgement about all the evacuation fosterings
made in Cambridge during the first evacuation. They found that
most went well and that only 8.2 per cent of evacuees had an
unhappy relationship with their foster parents. Issacs concludes
that this was 'a striking indication of the success of the evacuation
of these children'.

Subsequently, another piece of research by Drs Bannister and
Ravden also concerned evacuees in Cambridge and was later
published in the *British Journal of Psychology*. They studied
112 children, mainly in the age range 8–13 years, referred to the
Cambridge Child Guidance Clinic. The finding that 45 of the 112
were evacuees seemed to suggest that a very high proportion of
evacuees were in need of psychological help and that evacuation
was having an adverse effect on them. However, the researchers
continued that, by the time of referral, most evacuees had returned

home and that, in fact, the vast majority had not required psychological help. Those evacuee children left behind had tended to be those with severe difficulties whose parents could not cope with them.

Bannister and Ravden certainly considered that evacuation was a stress factor but that it most seriously affected those children who already had personal difficulties. They established that the children's problems—aggression, nervousness, delinquency—had the same causes in both evacuee and non-evacuee children, namely 'broken homes', 'over-protection' and 'unsatisfactory discipline'. The difficulties of the evacuee children stemmed back to their earlier childhood upbringing although the shock of evacuation may have aggravated them.

The findings that evacuation did not give birth to a generation of disturbed and delinquent youngsters surprised some experts who, before the war, had been making a connection between delinquency and broken homes. However, it is fallacious to compare delinquents with evacuees. The former, as identified in John Bowlby's study of juvenile thieves, tended to come from difficult, disturbed and interrupted home backgrounds, while the majority of evacuees came from ordinary, stable, mainly working-class homes. The former had to face parental rejection and blame while the latter knew that their separation was not the wish of their parents but was a product of the war. The broken homes of the delinquents were thus in no way like the separations enforced upon the evacuees and hence the effects on the children were entirely different. Not least, it must be remembered that most young children went with their mothers and that, even for the older ones, many were away for a short period, not the whole time of the war.

Evacuation certainly was a trauma which upset many children, particularly in the early stages, and which found expression in a minority of bed-wetting and upset behaviour. But these symptoms mostly faded over time.

Some evacuees were badly treated and some were very unhappy. But most appeared to have coped with evacuation while a number enjoyed the experience. Clearly some looked back upon evacuation as a positive time which they would not have missed.

Evacuation and education

Whether evacuated or staying in danger zones—and some children alternated between the two—many children had their schooling disrupted by the war.

The first evacuation occurred over a few days with the result that many of the reception areas were so taken up with finding billets that the organization of schooling for the newcomers took a low priority. Some children were out of school for weeks and when they did start were often in overcrowded classrooms in schools trying to cope not just with a surplus of evacuees but also a loss of experienced teachers to the armed forces and other war jobs. True, the children who came with school parties were accompanied by teachers but they too had to adapt to new surroundings, new colleagues and different equipment. The changes affected the local children as well as the evacuees. In Tiptree, Essex, the school population was doubled by the arrival of a whole children's home from London which moved into a large house, the Grove. They did not bring extra teachers and hence the existing staff had to deal with bulging classrooms, arranging new timetables and extra marking. As I have described elsewhere in 'Not Like Any Other Home' the outcome was some conflict with local children chanting,

Here comes the Grove,
All dressed in mauve,
Living on charity,
Huddling round a stove.

In one outburst, a teacher called them 'Grove scroungers'. The combination of being both the members of a children's home and evacuees was a stigma which some found hard to bear.

Although many children were evacuated as school units, they were often fostered over a wide area and so had to attend schools different from their friends. An exception occurred with a small number of what became called camp schools. The Manchester education department opened a camp at Somerford Hall in Congleton, Cheshire in April 1940. 'Camp' may give the wrong impression, for the 250 boys slept not in tents but in five wooden dormitories and were schooled in a new building. The camp was set in twenty-five acres, some of which the boys cultivated for their supplies of fruit and vegetables. The headmaster and seven teachers stressed the virtues of self-reliance and the outdoor life. It was much in demand and did not close until May 1945.

In Ilford, the Beal Secondary School was evacuated to Kenny-lands Camp. There the pupils lived together with the camp manager, Captain Mee, trying to establish the ethos of a public school. It attracted a number of visitors and much praise so that, when the war drew to a close, Mee campaigned for such schools to be established permanently to provide 'the robustness of health, the poise of character, the cultivation of personal talent and the habits of citizen-service, all of which are the real merits of the English public school.' *The Ilford Recorder* gave the proposal a cool reception while sensibly arguing that the education authority should maintain one residential establishment to give a wide number of pupils access to a residential stay. At the end of the war, the school's popular head, Mr W. Norman, brought the school back to Ilford and began to campaign, successfully, for grammar school status. The value of the camp schools was not any public school ethic but rather that they ensured continuity of education for older pupils.

It was continuity which many pupils lacked. Returning to the danger zones certainly did not provide that. In 1939, many authorities in those zones considered that bombing would start immediately and that all children would opt for evacuation. Consequently, schools were closed. But the numbers of those who took up offers of evacuation were less than anticipated, and others were coming home. Some education bodies responded by initiating classes in small groups in private homes.

In Sheffield, the kids called it 'housey-housey'. In Ilford, teachers also took children into parks for games. The Ilford Ratepayers' Associations were not impressed with this use of public money while the council conceded that the corporate aspect of school life was missing. By December 1939, the Director of Education estimated that 90 per cent of children had returned and that he wanted to open five of the Ilford schools. By February, the Government was urging the local authorities to restore compulsory education. The trouble was that many of the evacuated teachers had not come back while numerous schools, up to two-thirds in London and Manchester, had been taken over by the civil defence services. Certainly, some schools were re-opened but by March 1940, it was estimated that only a quarter of all children were in full-time education, a quarter in half-time, another quarter receiving some form of home tuition, and a final quarter not at school at all.

Just when the schools were preparing for the new autumn term of 1940, the real Blitz started and the trickle evacuation got under way. The schools system in the large cities broke down again so that by 1941, 92,000 children in London and 290,000 in England and Wales were without education. The officials did strive to make provision but when the next trek home occurred in 1942–43, they were handicapped by the damage wrought by bombs on school buildings— around 4,000 had been destroyed. The outcome was even bigger class sizes than before the war. In 1943, Liverpool had over 600 classes with more than fifty pupils in each. Glasgow, Sheffield, Bristol and Dudley also reported serious overcrowding.

In 1944, the V1s and V2s prompted the next exodus. In fact, many children remained in the danger zones although they were frequently absent from school as parents kept them at home in the face of daylight attacks. Others missed out when their families were moved following damage to their homes. Towards the end of 1944, the final march home was in progress. In Ilford it was estimated that 3,000 pupils, a quarter of the school roll, were back in attendance. More schools opened, so by mid-1945 attendance levels were almost back to normal.

One result of the breakdown of schooling in the danger zones, particularly in 1939–40 and during the Blitz, was that numerous children roamed around in what had been school time. A report from youth leaders in Peckham, quoted in *Borrowed Children* stated:

The fact that children are running wild is incontrovertible. We have not had so much trouble with organized gangs of children since we started here ten years ago.

In Ilford, in November 1939, a public meeting heard that the children 'are getting out of hand. There is no one who can control them like the teachers.' The Commission of the Churches reported that

a multitude of children lounged and roamed about the streets, tasting the perilous delights of idleness and indiscipline.

Angus Calder, not one to exaggerate, stated:

In the cities, over a million children were left to run wild. Children whose education was half complete took jobs. Others turned to hooliganism—so often were public air raid shelters wrecked by children that the authorities were compelled to keep them locked.

An example of the roaming child is found in Marian Hughes' autobiography, *No Cake, No Jam: A War-time Childhood*. She was living with her mother and siblings in war-time London where she ceased attending school. She writes:

Still not at school, Anthony and I roamed the streets from morning until night. We suffered little from hunger. What I stole I shared with Anthony. Mars was our favourite, for sweets were not yet rationed.
  The two of us found a new pursuit. The cinema! I loved the wonder of the movies, adored being transported to the jungle by Tarzan films, elated by the beat of the drum, the dancing of the natives, and terrified by the witch doctors. Revelling in the great dramas I fell in love for the first time—with Charles Laughton ... One of the cinemas we visited was the Blue Hall in the Edgware Road. I would climb through the ladies' lavatory window, slither on my belly, open an exit door for

Anthony, and, together in like manner, we'd creep through the
aisles, to surface on either side of an unfortunate couple,
adopting an air of belonging to them . . .
  We moved out. And moved again. Nineteen-forty-two
brought us to Westbourne Grove Terrace, off Westbourne Grove.
On one corner was the Timpo toy factory where they smelted lead
for toys. Greatly daring, Anthony would leap from our roof to
the roof of the factory, to steal brand-new boxed toys, which he
and I would sell to passers-by, who believed they were unwanted
Christmas presents. Almost opposite was Pritchard's which sold
bread and cakes, and became the unwitting and frequent
suppliers of wholesome nutrients.

Perhaps it is not surprising that between 1939–41 the number of
young people under the age of seventeen found guilty of breaking
the law in England and Wales rose by over a third.

The decline of full-time education, the over-crowding of
classrooms, the drop in attendances and the breaks in educational
continuity had an inevitable adverse effect on school standards and
pupils' achievements. Within the London County Council, a
comparison was made between the test results of thirteen- to
fourteen-year-olds in 1943 and those from 1924. In spelling,
arithmetic, history and geography, the levels of attainment were
markedly lower in 1943. Similar findings came from other
authorities. Confirmation of the downward trend came a few
years after the war when boys of war-time education began to
enter the army. Compared with those educated before the war,
they showed no decline in intelligence but a considerable drop in
scholastic achievements and a serious rise in numbers graded
educationally backward.

I reckon I was one who suffered educationally, for my first four
years of schooling were from 1941–45. I started in a hall bulging
with small children around single tables. Back in Ilford, I often did
not attend school when the raids were intense. In Cross Keys,
Herefordshire, I did not go at all as my mother refused to send us.
Back in Ilford while the V1s and V2s were falling I was again often
kept at home for safety and, when we did attend, we frequently sat

in the school shelter or got sent home early. Little wonder that I did poorly in those early years. I recall, soon after the war, being embarrassed at junior school because I could neither say the ABC nor tell the time. Curiously enough, I could read and became an avid reader of comics like the Wizard and Adventure. When my time was up at junior school, I was kept back a year and so parted from most of my mates. At least I was better than most of my new class members at football which was my major interest. I failed the eleven plus examination at my first attempt although I did pass it subsequently. I was not unusual. Evacuation and the bombing did blight the education of thousands.

Interestingly, the effect of the war on schooling drew public attention to the subject of education, attention which then led to demands for reform. One who took up the challenge was the remarkable Susan Lawrence. Born in 1871 to a rich family, she joined the Labour Party and in 1913 was elected to the London County Council. In 1923 she became MP for East Ham North and made her presence felt in the House of Commons with her fierce upper-class voice, the wearing of a monocle, and a passionate identification with the poor. Education was one of her main interests and in January 1940—in her late sixties—she wrote a Labour Party pamphlet, *The Children's Welfare in War Time*. She started by saying that the first casualty of the war had been universal, compulsory education and continued,

> *We have indeed to go back to the 1870s to find the present state of affairs in some of our great cities. Then, and not since then, we heard of hundreds of thousands of children running wild because there were no schools in which to locate them.*

Of course, it was working-class children, not those who attended private schools, who suffered. Lawrence wanted to reverse this by arguing that the war presented opportunities for improving state education. So she advocated not just a return to school but the implementation of the promise to raise the school leaving age and the use of schools for improved distribution of milk, food and medical treatment. The aim, she said, was to end the war 'with a generation better physically equipped than any we have known'. Further, Lawrence—and her colleagues—argued that the time was ripe for introducing free secondary and higher education. Susan Lawrence thus fired the first shots in what became a battle of debate about education that continued throughout the war. This process, of the evacuation opening public gaze to the limitations of social services and then leading on to campaigns for improvements, was to be repeated for other welfare services. So, the evacuation meant varying experiences, negative and positive, for the children concerned. It was also to have a collective effect on welfare as will be developed in the next chapter.

5 The Response to Evacuation

Evacuation was initiated by central government which made policy decisions and authorized payments for foster parents. Local authorities implemented the conveying and reception of the evacuees. However, once the evacuees were in place, many social problems arose which required responses from the social services.

Social Services in 1939

The question of whether the services could cope with the new demands created by the movements of masses of children and mothers depend upon their scope and quality in 1939. So what was the nature of welfare at the beginning of the war?

The care of socially needy people in Britain had long been rooted in the Poor Law which dated back to the Elizabethan Relief Act of 1601. The later Poor Law Amendment Act of 1834 laid down practices which were to dominate for the next century. It stipulated that able-bodied destitute people should receive help only on condition of entering a workhouse wherein conditions should be so severe as to deter applicants. The result was a stigma imposed on inmates who were regarded as social failures and a fear imposed on outsiders that they might finish up in the workhouse. The stigma and fear suited the Guardians—elected by ratepayers of the parish to oversee the local Poor Law—for they saw their main aim as to keep down costs.

The Poor Law provoked great controversy and changes did occur. In 1892, George Lansbury, the Christian socialist, was elected one of the first working-class Guardians. Elected with him in Poplar, was Will Crooks who entered, as a Guardian, into the very room in the workhouse where years before he had been received as a pauper child. As I have recounted in my book *Good Old George: The Life of George Lansbury*, the reformers struggled on two fronts: both reform from within the establishments and reform without—in legislation.

As Guardians, they attempted to humanize the workhouses from within, improving the diet, abolishing uniforms, sacking cruel and corrupt staff. When Lansbury became chairman of the Poor Law residential school, he abolished the seven-course dinners which the children served to the Guardians, introduced sport to the curriculum, and sent the children out to ordinary day schools. It became a model residential establishment and, when visited by royalty, the children broke ranks chanting, 'Good old George, Good old George.'

In addition, Lansbury and Crooks both became MPs. They joined with others to extend out-relief—the giving of small grants to allow certain categories, like widows, to remain in their own homes.

Lansbury wanted the Poor Law abolished. This never happened in his lifetime but, in 1929, its administration was removed from the Guardians and placed with the Public Assistance Committees of local authorities—the county and county borough councils—under the overall control of the Ministry of Health. However, for all the re-organization and re-naming, the spirit of and the fear of the workhouse remained. In the 1930s, children who were in the care of Public Assistance Committees and who passed scholarships to grammar schools were often prohibited from proceeding on the grounds that the fees would be an unjustified use of public money. Poor people were still terrified of finishing up in what they still called the workhouse. Their fear was not misplaced, for in 1939 Public Assistance institutions contained nearly 100,000 inmates.

But the first decade of the century did also see the beginning of services which, in the long run, were to enable more people to cope outside of institutions. These services were not primarily intended as such: for example, the establishment of the school medical service and the feeding of children in elementary schools arose partly from national worries about the poor health of recruits to the army. The famous Liberal reforming Government continued with the introduction of old age pensions for a limited number of those over seventy and followed this with the National Insurance Act which set up provision quite separate from the Poor Law. National Insurance entailed contributions from the State, employers and workers, with the latter gaining access to medical treatment, sickness benefits and unemployment pay. However, the scheme covered only a small part of the working population and for a limited time period. Its scope was gradually widened; none the less, in 1934 the Government had to create the Unemployment Assistance Board, an indication that the problems of unemployment were so massive that central intervention was necessary. Under pressure from radical politicians, Government also gave local authorities more powers to extend their services. Most important was the growth of council housing: 121,658 dwellings were constructed in 1939.

Statutory services by no means dominated the welfare services. Private and voluntary insurance, such as that run by friendly societies, were well patronized by those in regular employment. The national child care societies, such as Dr Barnardo's, the National Children's Home and Orphanage, and the Waifs and Strays Society (later The Children's Society), maintained over one thousand children's homes, and so looked after as many children as the statutory establishments. Further, the gradual expansion of statutory welfare suffered setbacks during the economic recession of the late 1920s and 1930s when unemployment escalated to three million and the trade gap widened.

A few economists, particularly John Maynard Keynes, argued that the Government should maintain the incomes of poor people in order to increase demand at home so as to strengthen British industry. But most private employers wanted public expenditure, taxes and wages cut in order to make industry more competitive. Ironically it was the minority Labour Government, led by Ramsay

MacDonald, which faced the worst of the crisis. When its leaders agreed to massive economies, several Ministers, including Lansbury, rebelled. MacDonald resigned in 1931 but then formed a National Government. In the ensuing general election it overwhelmingly defeated Labour which was reduced to fifty-two seats.

It can be seen that the Welfare State did not arrive suddenly in 1945. It was evolving slowly throughout the early decades of the twentieth century and, by the 1930s, a framework of National Insurance, Education and Public Assistance services were in place. However, they were generally under-funded and the economic depression had led to cut-backs. Indeed, during the 1930s, National Insurance payments were cut by 10 per cent, the Unemployment Assistance Board imposed stringent means tests and local authorities slowed their growth with some even abolishing school meals. Moreover, the political party most in favour of promoting welfare provision, the Labour Party, looked incapable of winning a general election.

By 1939, the limitations and weaknesses of the social services can be itemized as follows:

National Insurance. Cover for health, unemployment and pensions was limited in scope—unskilled workers, women and children were largely excluded.

The result was that, on any one day, over one million people still had to receive help from the Public Assistance departments, which, to members of the working class, still meant the Poor Law.

Local authority housing. Although this was growing, it was still very limited in numbers. The majority of citizens on low incomes resided in privately-rented, poor-quality dwellings.

Health Service. Only insured workers, not their wives and children, received free treatment from general practitioners. Even then, they were known as the 'panel' patients, still regarded as inferior to those who paid the doctors for treatment. Most hospitals were run by local authorities, often with insufficient budgets, or by voluntary bodies who frequently depended upon flag days to finance them.

Uneven provision of services. Local authority provision in health and welfare varied enormously between areas. The numbers of health visitors in some authorities was one per hundred children, while in others it was one per thousand. Similar differences occurred in the distribution of maternity services and child welfare clinics which tended to concentrate only on children aged one and under. Day nurseries and nursery schools—both new ventures—had places for only 14,000 children in England and Wales.

State education. This ensured elementary schooling for 5–14-year-olds and benefited from the growth of a dedicated teaching profession. But the system was under-resourced with more than one in three classes containing over forty pupils. The Government had decided to raise the school leaving age to fifteen but had not implemented it.

Even if they passed scholarships, few working-class children went on to secondary education and even fewer to university. The affluent sent their children to private schools in which the privileged public schools dominated entrance to Oxbridge, the professions and politics.

Care of deprived children, the elderly, and the mentally ill. There were no local authority departments in these areas. Social workers were few in number and there was little training for them or for residential staff.

Arthur Marwick in his book *The Home Front* summed up the position on the outbreak of war:

> *Although the social services had been expanded during and after the First World War, they still contained many gaps. In general, they were confined to the working class, and, in many cases, were only available after an applicant had undergone a strict Means Test.*

Such was the welfare provision which was to be tested by the evacuation.

The voluntary response

Evacuation removed children and young mothers from the danger zones. In so doing it also provoked numerous social difficulties. Foster mothers complained about the behaviour and clothing of the evacuees and that their allowances were insufficient. The mothers who had accompanied young children experienced loneliness, isolation and difficulties in obtaining food and clothing. Almost immediately concerns were expressed both about the inadequacies of medical and welfare services. The influx of thousands of children and mothers meant that existing hospitals, welfare clinics and maternity units and their doctors, nurses and health visitors just could not cope. In Dartington, Devon, for instance, the arrival of hundreds of children just became too much for the small number of GPs in the village. Even when medical services could be given, questions arose over who was financially responsible for the evacuees. In short, both the limitations of the distribution and of the methods of paying for health and welfare were brought into focus.

Further, worries were voiced about the health of evacuees. The term 'skinnies' had some justification in that evacuee children, mothers and babies were clearly under-fed compared with the people with whom they were staying. This fact should not have been a complete surprise. Pre-war research by Sir John Boyd Orr had demonstrated that the diet of the poorest 10 per cent of the population was deficient in nearly all known vitamins, with the result that its members were more vulnerable to illness and death than other sections of the nation. The difference in 1939 was that their ill-health became visible as they were transported from urban to rural areas.

Initially, the statutory authorities were slow to respond. Central government, still ruled by the Treasury, was reluctant to take on extra welfare costs. It even refused a Ministry of Health request for £10,000 to help immediate necessitous cases amongst evacuees so that they would not have to approach Public Assistance. The local authorities disagreed amongst themselves as to whether reception or evacuation zones should pay for additional costs. As happens in so many cases, it was the voluntary bodies who acted first. Charitable bodies collected second-hand clothes and money for new supplies. The National Union of Teachers donated £1,000 while clothes arrived from the USA. In Cambridge, concern was expressed as to how evacuee children would spend their spare time. After meetings, came quick action. The Women's Voluntary Services appointed a member to organize out-of-school activities: four play centres were set up on Saturday mornings by a worker from the London Play Centre Movement. Some teachers, mainly evacuee ones, initiated after-school clubs. The churches too were heavily involved in most reception areas with the Commission of the Churches reporting as follows:

> *There was an almost universal opening up of services and Sunday Schools to evacuees, and in many cases all youth organisations were thrown open to them. Sunday School attendances advanced in some places on a most extensive scale. One place recorded trebled numbers, one an increase of 300, and one the creation of two new schools for half a hundred each. Some churches clearly took more pains than others. In Sevenoaks a joint committee of young people visited evacuees personally, in order to fit them into the different Sunday Schools. Other districts also carried out visiting, and others distributed leaflets.*

The participation of churches was also noted in Cambridge, although it was reported that evacuees were not easily incorporated into existing scout groups. Their attendance at uniformed movements seemed to flourish best when their arrival stirred the creation of new troops or corps. As the Cambridge survey sadly concluded, 'So far London and Cambridge children tend to remain apart at school and play.'

Local organizations also responded to the needs of young mothers. Soon after their arrival in 1939, a number of community associations and women's groups opened local halls where evacuee mothers could meet together, have a snack, receive advice about the whereabouts of clinics and sometimes have a break from their children. Again the churches were involved, for they often possessed the physical plant—church halls—and volunteers motivated to help. The Commission of the Churches estimated that two-thirds of churches in the reception areas made some provision for evacuee children or mothers or both. It gave one example as follows:

> *One country vicar was already a billeting officer and his wife a member of the WVS, but they cleared out the ground floor of the vicarage ... and established and themselves ran a day nursery and nursery school, and a canteen where over a hundred children were given lunch daily.*

Official responses

The voluntary action was an indication that evacuees really did require special welfare provision. Whether the statutory bodies felt shamed by the speedy voluntary response is impossible to say. What is certain is that the authorities did become worried about the number of evacuees who were returning to the danger zones. It therefore decided to take steps to ease the lot of evacuees. In November 1939 the Ministry of Health, having initially said that evacuee families in need of clothing would have to apply to Public Assistance Departments, that is the Poor Law, then reversed the decision by making small amounts of money available to directors of education to deal directly with needy cases.

Titmuss, in *Problems of Social Policy*, recorded that 'This small grant was, in effect, the beginning of a new social service.' He meant that central government was now providing money for a local authority to help poor people without going through the stigma of the Poor Law means test. With the precedent set, the Government then made money available for social centres, clubs and canteens for the evacuee mothers. The war in general and evacuation in particular was pushing both central and local government into extending the scope and nature of its welfare services.

Simultaneously, the authorities had to take seriously the problems in foster homes. As mentioned, the allowances paid to foster homes were eventually, if modestly, increased. More noteworthy, most reception authorities strengthened the work and role of the billeting officers by recruiting paid and voluntary visitors to call on the foster parents in order to check upon the well-being of the children and to discuss problems with the foster parents. The Ministry of Health, through its regional welfare officers, took on an advisory role and recommended that the children be seen at least once a month. It is not known if this guidance was acted upon but it is clear that a new kind of child care service was developing within the local authorities. The visitors were mainly untrained and out of their depth in counselling foster parents whose children were displaying severe problems. A number of reception authorities sought more skilled help from child guidance experts.

Child guidance had its origins in the USA and was imported into Britain in the late 1920s. Its aim, to cite Susan Issacs, one of its leading exponents, was 'restoring and fostering satisfactory development in the less stable child.' It developed a team approach involving a psychiatrist, educational psychologist and psychiatric social workers. Using psychoanalytic concepts, the team would assess a child's problems and then undertake treatment, often with the psychiatrist concentrating on the child and the social workers on the parents.

Meanwhile, the London School of Economics had established a mental health course as a professional training for social workers. Before war broke out, some of the graduates of the course foresaw that evacuation would provoke severe problems for some children of the kind which would require their kind of expertise. Five organizations, the Central Association for Mental Welfare, the Child Guidance Council, the National Council for Mental Hygiene, the Association of Mental Health Workers, and the Association of Psychiatric Social Workers, came together to form the Mental Health Emergency Committee in 1939. It then drew up a register of qualified workers, persuaded the Government not to conscript them, and circulated local authorities with the likely value of child guidance work in the event of evacuation. Thus, at the very point in the autumn of 1939 when reception areas were facing problems in foster homes, the offer of skilled help was at hand.

The small county of Huntingdonshire had its rural population of 56,000 swollen by 6,000 evacuees. As elsewhere, a number of foster parents felt unable to cope with their children and one billeting officer found three dumped on his doorstep. But the problems had been anticipated and the assistant Medical Officer of Health co-operated with the Women's Voluntary Service to secure the appointments of two psychiatric social workers and an educational psychologist. Between September 1939 and February 1940, 131 evacuee children and eleven local children were referred to this team. The social workers made regular visits to the foster homes which they deemed to have the most severe problems. In a few cases, children did have to be removed but mostly the support and understanding received from the social workers enabled the foster parents to cope. Simultaneously, the team established four centres to which foster parents could bring children. At these the foster parents received advice while the children participated in group play sessions and, if necessary, direct treatment from a visiting psychiatrist. Lastly, they founded a residential home for twenty children whose problems could not be contained within foster homes.

Cambridge, like Huntingdonshire, also took a large number of evacuees in a short space of time. It was fortunate in having a general hospital which not only had psychiatric staff but also the beginning of a child guidance clinic. Moreover, the mental health course from the London School of Economics was evacuated to Cambridge. The authorities were thus well placed to quickly put a child guidance service for evacuees into operation. The procedure was that billeting officers and visitors could refer cases to the psychiatric social workers at the clinic. During the first evacuation, 48 per cent of the referrals concerned bed-wetting; 16 per cent stealing; 8 per cent quarrelsome behaviour. The social workers prepared reports and the clinic team decided what, if any, action was necessary. Of 130 children seen at the clinic, it was decided that 39 per cent required psychiatric treatment; 26 per cent could be helped via the social workers;

18 per cent needed a change of foster parents; 15 per cent should be admitted to an emergency hostel; and 2 per cent needed an open air school. Subsequently, Issacs explained that 68 per cent of the children did improve. A hostel was started in February 1940 and took twenty-five children 'most of them quite seriously unstable and in need of the most patient and understanding handling and a really secure background.'

The examples of Huntingdonshire and Cambridge were followed by some other authorities. Glasgow had possessed four child guidance clinics in 1939 and, during the war, it established three more to help evacuees in the west of Scotland. Particularly noteworthy was the opening, in September 1940, of the Nerston Residential Clinic with five qualified staff in residence. The clinic took thirty-eight children with very severe problems, children who had been through several foster homes and who displayed violence, instability and extreme difficulties which required specialist help. The aim of the establishment, in the words of Boyd in his *Evacuation in Scotland*, was 'to establish a family unit and at-tempt to carry out the instructions usually given to parents by the clinicians.' The numbers were probably too large and the staff were stretched to the limits to maintain control in the early days when there was much stealing and even outbursts of hysteria. On one occasion, a ten-year-old, clad only in pyjama trousers, led his followers, shouting 'The spirit of the Lord is upon you.' A staff member, perhaps abandoning some of his enlightened principles, intervened with, 'My hand will be upon you in three minutes if you're not in your bed.' Gradually order was imposed within a framework of security and affection. The staff gave particular attention to promoting the children's academic achievements as a means of building up their self-confidence while individual treatment was also available for those with special, psychological needs. The children stayed for between six to eighteen months and of the more than 200 children who were resident during the war years only a few failed to improve.

Also in Scotland, the Peebleshire County Council and the Society of Friends co-operated to found Barnes House as a hostel for boys showing difficulties in foster homes. Led by David Wills, who was to become a foremost figure in the world of residential care, it aimed to provide a family environment, security and discipline without recourse to corporal punishment. The emphasis was put on staff and children sharing responsibility for behaviour. A social worker liaised with the foster parents, for the intention was to return children to them. Wills' methods won a great deal of attention and the work at Barnes House continued after the war for children who displayed problems in their own homes.

The number of homes—or hostels as they were often called—arising out of the evacuation rose to over 700. Not all ran well: inappropriate staffing appointments were made; and some authorities used them as depositories for any difficult children whether they were evacuees or not. The hostel described by Laurie Laken in the last chapter may well have been more typical than those in Cambridge, Glasgow and Peebleshire. At this point the Ministry of Health, again through its social welfare advisors, began to exercise a valuable role of guidance. It specified that the hostels were for evacuees and that the main aim was to help the children so that they could settle into foster homes. Most homes were intended to be short-term but provision was made for some to specialize in long-term care and treatment. Qualified staff were difficult if not impossible to find but it was emphasized that care should be taken in appointments with efforts made to find experienced workers.

During the 1930s, residential services for children were in stagnation. Responsibility was fragmented between voluntary bodies and local authorities with the latter possibly having homes run by the Public Assistance, Health and Education Departments. Some residential establishments did contain dedicated staff who did their best for children but generally residential care was characterized by a lack of skilled staff locally and an absence of leadership nationally. The evacuation served as a catalyst which pushed both local and central government into action. In the face of numbers of children who could not be contained within foster homes, the local authorities, often in co-operation with voluntary bodies, had to provide residential care. As such care was expanded over the country, the Ministry of Health felt obliged not only to authorize such developments but also to give it some shape and uniformity. It should be emphasized that the numbers of children requiring residential provision were just a small minority of the evacuees. Further, the evidence was that while their problems may have been brought to the fore by the evacuation, they actually sprang from earlier difficulties at home. The last point was an important one, for it meant that evacuation had unearthed a childcare need which would not go away with the end of the war. Yet the childcare experience gained had the potential for continuing better services after the war.

Health and welfare

One of the most worrying problems for the reception zones in 1939 was whether they could cope with the pregnant women who were being evacuated. Being rural areas, their maternity facilities tended to be scattered over wide distances. The problem was anticipated but action was held back over the issue of costs. Who would pay for the extra maternity provision? The reception authorities considered it the responsibility of the authorities from whom the mothers came and vice versa. Not until 29 August did the Ministry of Health guarantee payment. By wonders of improvisation, the health departments in the reception areas had 1,003 extra beds ready by 2 September although it was uncertain who would staff them. By October, 3,700 beds were in place (some in 137 extra maternity homes) and 2,881 confinements took place.

Problems still continued. Did the financial arrangements also apply to evacuees who were outside the official schemes and had come privately? The Ministry of Health eventually decided they did. All the time arrangements were being made for the drafting in of extra doctors, nurses and medical equipment. Somehow it happened. But once all the services were functioning, many evacuees began returning home with the result that some pregnant women then had difficulties in finding maternity beds in the danger zones. The Ministry of Health advised against dismantling the new provisions, for it predicted that once bombing started the evacuation would re-commence. It was proved right and, when the Blitz sparked off the trickle evacuation, the reception areas were ready with adequate maternity facilities.

Once the babies were born, the mothers needed welfare clinics and health visitors. The needs of evacuee mothers were greater than before for now they lacked the support of husbands, relatives and neighbours. Between 1939–44, the number of welfare clinics or centres increased by over 600. Interestingly, Titmuss reports that their growing reputation also prompted much greater attendance by local middle-class mothers. These developments created extra demand for health visitors both to staff the centres and to visit mothers with small children. The problem was that personnel with nursing qualifications were wanted for a whole variety of war-time tasks and jobs. None the less, local authorities did manage to push up their numbers of health visitors although those employed by voluntary bodies went into decline.

The war years witnessed a three-fold increase in illegitimate births. Pregnant, unmarried evacuees were accepted into maternity units in reception areas alongside other women. Difficulties arose after birth for the billeting officers found it hard to find households willing to take them in. Consequently, some young mothers and their babies had to go from the maternity units into Public Assistance institutions. But they were not welcome, for Public Assistance, still guided by Poor Law practice, insisted that any costs had to be paid by their home authorities. In Somerset, one dispute resulted in the Public Assistance Department putting two young mothers and their babies on the train back to London. The Ministry of Health was worried on two grounds: it did not want evacuees returning to the danger zones, and further, a new spirit was emerging that did not want any evacuees treated by the Poor Law and which argued that unmarried mothers should receive the same services as other evacuees. The result was a new drive to find them places within the reception communities with some health departments appointing social workers to work with unmarried mothers, and thus developing another service which had hardly existed before the war.

Meantime, steps were also being taken to meet the nutritional needs of mothers and children. Shortage of certain foods in the initial period of the war, evidence of higher infant death rates in 1939–40, a rise in cases of tuberculosis, and the revelations about the health of evacuees, all combined to move the Government to action. It increased grant aid to local authorities to improve and extend the provision of school meals and school milk. A circular of 1940 stated, 'There is no question of capacity to pay: we may find the children of well-to-do parents and the children of the poor suffering alike from an inability to get the food they need.' The outcome was an upsurge in the provision of meals and milk. In July 1940, 130,000 school dinners were being taken each day in England and Wales. By 1945 it was 1,650,000, with 14 per cent being free and the rest costing four pence. By 1945, 73 per cent of school children were taking the two-thirds of a pint of milk offered to them each school day.

Simultaneously, the National Milk scheme provided a pint of milk daily for all expectant and nursing mothers and all children under the age of five at the price of 2d a pint or free for those on low incomes. The scheme and its costs were borne by the Ministry of Food. In 1941 came the Vitamin Welfare scheme, granting free orange juice and cod-liver oil to expectant mothers and small children (with vitamins A and D as an alternative). Within a short space of time, the trend of declining local authority provision of school meals had been reversed and a vast scheme of food supplements put into place. The Government had acted on an unprecedented scale and one of the factors making them do so was the evacuation.

Day care

Just as the health needs of evacuees widened into a concern for the nutrition of all mothers and children, so their immediate needs for day care soon merged with a drive to provide nursery care for war-time working mothers all over the country.

Marjory Allen, Lady Allen of Hurtwood, was one of a number who observed the plight of evacuee mothers:

dragging their little children with them wherever they went. Lonely and overstrained, it is small wonder that many of them lost heart. Small wonder, too, that the under-fives often suffered from lack of suitable food, lack of quiet rest and lack

*of opportunity for exploratory play. They urgently needed a
place of their own, where friction was reduced to a minimum,
where prohibitions were not all-important and where they could
make a noise and exercise their natural curiosity without
troubling their mothers, foster-mothers or landladies.*

As mentioned above, some voluntary bodies had established
Centres for evacuee mothers and their small children. These were
never sufficient in number and eventually the Government did
respond both to their example and the pleas of people like Lady
Allen by encouraging local authorities to set up similar centres.
But it could be hard going, as Lucy Faithfull found when she
started trying to set up local authority centres in the Midlands:

*We ran into difficulties because we could not subscribe to the
high standards demanded by the doctors and educationalists for
the nurseries. I set up several groups, they were more like today's
playgroups, but the doctors and educationalists closed some of
them, not realizing what it meant to the women to have one or
two hours free. An enormous number of professional women had
gone into the forces so we could not get qualified staff.*

Lady Allen would have agreed with the case for qualified staff
but not with the lack of action to remedy it. She used her
considerable skills as a publicist to draw attention to the needs of
the under-fives and found some receptive ears at Whitehall where
the officials with responsibility for evacuation were still keen to
provide facilities to persuade evacuee mothers to stay in the
country. Their case was then strengthened by a growing need to
make provision for the children of women working in factories
both in the reception and danger zones. They still met some
opposition from county medical officers of health who considered
that the woman's place was in the home and, in addition, from
some psychologists who were worried about the effects on young
children of separating them from their mothers for long hours. But
the demand for women war-time workers in factories, on the land,
and in civil defence posts grew apace.

In 1941, the Ministry of Health took overall responsibility for day nurseries and stimulated two kinds. One was the part-time nursery, suitable for the children of evacuee mothers: the other was full-time, suitable for working mothers. Flushed with 100 per cent grants from Government, the local authorities acted quickly and even overcame the staffing problems. By the end of November 1941, nearly two hundred new nurseries had been opened, with another 500 in the planning pipeline. By 1944, more than 106,000 young children in England and Wales were in 1,559 nurseries; there were 6,227 places taken in nursery schools and 28,650 children in 784 nursery classes. In addition, some 102,940 children had places in reception classes at elementary schools.

The needs of the evacuee mothers had initiated the demand for provision for the under-fives. But their lobby had been overtaken by that for working mothers all over the country. Lady Allen, too, was not entirely pleased by developments. The main thrust had been in the provision of what were day nurseries, which looked after the health care of children but which she regarded as deficient in educational content. She was also of the belief that children under the age of three should only be parted from their mothers for part of the day before proceeding to nursery education at three. She worked with others in the nursery education lobby which gained success when the 1944 Education Act contained a provision putting responsibility for nursery education onto local authorities. But whether day nurseries or nursery education, the war years did see a massive growth in day care provision.

The importance of evacuation

Both central and local government and voluntary bodies responded to welfare needs stimulated by the movement of millions of evacuees. What was the effect of these responses on the nature and extent of state welfare? Opinions differ. Richard Titmuss, who saw the home front at first hand and studied it on behalf of the Government, producing *Problems of Social Policy*, was sure that they changed the practice of welfare and introduced new welfare principles. More recently, John Macnicol in his chapter 'The effect of the evacuation of schoolchildren on official attitudes to state intervention' in *British Society in the Second World War*, casts doubts on the importance of the evacuation on two grounds. One is that some welfare changes were already being planned before the evacuation: for example, the Government had announced its wish to increase the consumption of milk; and the powers of the Poor Law were being eroded throughout the century. The other is that issues of principle were not strong and that policy arose from expediency: thus the means test for school milk was abolished not because of a belief in universal services but simply because it was inconvenient to adminster it to thousands of families.

Macnicol is right to note that some changes had been mooted. But it was evacuation that acted as the catalyst to bring them into reality, to push the Government into making school meals and milk into a national service on a scale that probably would not have happened. Moreover, the growth of nurseries and welfare clinics, the introduction of welfare foods, the development of child guidance and the escalation of residential care for disturbed children, were features which certainly were not being planned before evacuation. Whatever the reasons for maximizing these services—and certainly expediency, the response to a crisis, was one—their very scale and importance stimulated new public thinking about welfare. Consequently, as Titmuss shows throughout his profound account of Britain during the war, welfare principles came to the fore as never before.

Of course, a multitude of factors affected the course of welfare during the war years. I estimate that the evacuation did have a profound influence for two main reasons. First, the evacuation revealed, to the public at large, the weaknesses of the welfare system. In the late 1930s, for all the modifications, the British social services were still in the grip of the Poor Law. It was not just that the Public Assistance Departments were the direct heir of Poor Law legislation, applying means tests and maintaining harsh institutions. It was also that its policy of what Titmuss calls 'localism' was taken on board by other local authority services. Localism meant that departments tried to restrict services to established residents of their locality. If services were given to outsiders or temporary residents then charges were placed upon the area from where they had come. Evacuation was to expose the inadequacies and expense of this system.

During the first evacuation, the Government soon accepted that it should take on financial responsibility for the maternity costs of evacuees. It had to act quickly because reception and sending authorities were immediately arguing over the costs of even this service. Thereafter, the local authorities which were looking after the evacuees billed their home authorities for general hospital, mental hospital, Public Assistance and other services, including some school services, which the evacuees had to use. Arguments broke out over some of the bills: Cambridge County Council charged the London County Council for dental treatment provided under the schools medical service but the latter refused to pay and argued it was a central government responsibility. Similar disputes arose over the costs of immunizing evacuee children against diphtheria. And what of evacuees who had lived in several local authorities prior to evacuation? Voluminous correspondence ensued with an army of clerks sending invoices, paying bills, arguing cases and claiming refunds. The cost of administration may well have exceeded the amount of money it raised. Evacuation showed that the Poor Law practice of localism was incompatible with a mobile society.

Evacuation also revealed the variability of local authority welfare provision. In their official investigation of the social services during the war, *Studies in the Social Services*, Sheila Ferguson and Hilde Fitzgerald wrote:

The network of maternity services which covered the country at the outbreak of war had one primary characteristic: it was strong in some and weak in other places. The more advanced and wealthier authorities provided services of a high standard; in poor and backward areas few facilities were available. Country districts were often badly served, and many a countrywoman's only alternative to a home confinement was the Public Assistance institution with its stigma and poor standards. Even within towns, where the services were numerically adequate, quality varied from one district to another, with the poor, thickly populated industrial areas often at a disadvantage. One of the most disquieting features of all was the maldistribution of obstetric skill. In some parts of the country specialist advice in childbirth was almost unobtainable.

Similar variation concerned general hospitals. Evacuees might find themselves close to well-equipped local authority hospitals or modern voluntary ones. More likely, as Calder explained in *The People's War*, they would find themselves in

bare, overcrowded, large wards, cheerless, uncomfortable day rooms and primitive facilities for nursing . . . institutions where the ratio of patients to trained nurses is sixty or over.

The same variations could be found in welfare clinics, nurseries, numbers of GPs and health visitors, nursery schools, and size of school classes. Of course, the maldistribution of resources existed before evacuation but the sudden arrival of thousands of evacuees brought it before the public. Suddenly there were sick people who could not be found a nearby hospital, mothers discovering that the welfare clinic was twenty miles away, children being turned away from bulging schoolrooms. The lesson drawn was that access to local authority welfare services depended not on need but on the chance of where one happened to live. The implication was that if greater equality of access was desirable then central government would have to be more involved in two ways: by setting down guidelines as to the necessary quality and quantity of services—and it started to do this in regard to residential hostels; and by ensuring that local authorities had sufficient finance—as it did in regard to maternity provision.

The new demands associated with the influx of evacuees also highlighted the problem of the fragmentation of services. Lady Allen found it difficult to pin down who was responsible for day care for small children. At local level, was it the Health Department or the Education Department? At central government level was it the Ministry of Health, the Board of Education or even the Home Office? In addition, there were the voluntary bodies and, in the early days of the war it had been the national childcare societies, particularly the Waifs and Strays Society which had led the way. But most of all, as with the variation of service, it was maternity services which were most fragmented. Ferguson and Fitzherbert, published in 1954, made the obvious point that if co-ordination was needed anywhere it was in ante- and postnatal services. They continued:

> *It was for this reason that the division of the country's medical services into several unco-ordinated parts—medical practice, hospitals and local public services—was felt more painfully in the maternity services than anywhere else. The great difference in the standard and extent of the provision in different areas magnified still further the effect of divided rule. In England and Wales over 400 welfare authorities with permissive powers provided such services as health visiting and clinics. There were 188 supervisory authorities for domiciliary midwifery. Two different types of hospital, municipal and voluntary, maintained the beds for institutional confinements and usually their own ante- and postnatal clinics. The health visitor, the domiciliary midwife and the hospital, all supposed to work hand in hand, were often responsible to different authorities or boards. The medical officer at the local clinic was cut off from the institutional services and never saw a confinement. The general medical practitioner, unless he was called in privately or happened to be employed by a local authority, did not come into the picture at all, except in domiciliary emergency cases, if he was prepared to attend them. More often than not, when he was called in by a midwife, he saw the patient for the first time and knew nothing about her history.*

Little wonder that the pregnant evacuee mother arriving in a country area found it difficult to understand the system. At least back home, she had been in a tightly knit, if over-crowded, neighbourhood, where the services were well-known and near at hand. Fragmentation was wasteful of resources of welfare agencies, made coordination difficult for staff, and defied the understanding of users.

Local authorities did provide some excellent services run by dedicated staff. Yet, they could not cope when faced with thousands of mothers separated from their home support systems, with children vulnerable because apart from their parents, and with families whose poverty was brought into the open. Evacuation, as Angus Calder put it, 'exposed the inadequacy of Britain's social services both in town and country.' It thus raised questions of equity. Should evacuees and their like have the same access to services as other people? And it raised issues of control. How could a better distribution of resources and more efficient co-ordination come about? Could local authorities achieve these ends under central government guidance or should the latter administer them itself? Such questions were brought into the open during the evacuation.

The evacuation also had a strong influence on the course of welfare in that it stimulated a great expansion of statutory provision. The needs of evacuees directly led to the growth of maternity facilities, centres for mothers, welfare clinics, day nurseries, child guidance services and residential hostels. The exposure of the ill health of the evacuees combined with other factors to expand the provision of school meals and milk and the establishment of the welfare foods scheme. The expansion was the more remarkable in that it followed hard on the accepted wisdom of retrenchment of the 1930s. Moreover, it occurred not under a Labour Government but initially under a National one led by Chamberlain and then under a Coalition one led by Churchill who had previously warned against the dangers of collective welfare.

The wartime welfare expansion did not have to be permanent. Like the conscripted army, it could have been dismantled. But the new services clearly met existing needs and hence mostly became a permanent part of welfare. Consider maternity facilities: before the war, only a third of births could take place in maternity beds. The increase following evacuation pushed this figure up to over 50 per cent. Moreover, the new units were distributed more fairly across the country and reached, as Ferguson and Fitzgerald make clear, those parts where maternity provision had been most neglected. With an anticipated baby boom after the war, there could be no going back. Consider nursing: the new maternity units and the needs of hospitals in war-time created a tremendous demand for nurses. At a time of nursing shortage, the Ministry of Health stepped in to set up its Nursing Division in 1941 and evolved a national nursing policy. It strove to distribute nurses where they were most needed and even coped with fluctuating demand as evacuees moved between reception areas and home areas. The maximisation of nursing skills was so successful that it seemed foolish to change after the war. Consider the welfare clinics and centres whose numbers rose significantly: they became so popular with a wide range of users that there could be no question of going back to the 1939 position.

Lastly, consider the outcome of the increased welfare services. In 1939, the infant mortality rate was 51 per 1,000 live births in England and Wales and 69 in Scotland. By 1945 it was 46 and 56 respectively. In addition, in 1944 the Ministry of Health announced that the neo-mortality rate and the maternal mortality rate were the lowest on record. Beyond doubt, these improvements sprang from a combination of better maternity services and the more healthy diets associated with the war-time health schemes. Mention too must be made of the improved immunization campaign, often based on the new welfare clinics, which involved seven million children being immunized free of charge and led to a dramatic halving of deaths by diphtheria. The success of the new welfare was clear to all.

The war, conscription, bombing, evacuation—all led to enormous distress and suffering in Britain. Paradoxically, it also resulted in expanded and improved welfare services which improved the diet, the safety, the health and well-being of many mothers and children. The improvements were obvious and appreciated and there was no desire to put the clock back. At the end of the war, the number of day nursery places was put into reverse as conscripted men returned to jobs which many women had been doing. But the other local services remained in place. Evacuation had brought about permanent change in welfare. It was increasingly accepted not only that local authorities should make more provision but also that more services should be without a means test, that more should be used by the whole community, and that central government should have an active role in ensuring the quality of services and the proper distribution of welfare resources at local level.

6 Desperate straits to Welfare State

In 1940 British forces were driven out of Europe while Britain was Blitzed by the *Luftwaffe*. The nation expected and Hitler planned invasion. Desperate straits. Yet, within less than a decade, not only was the war over but the same Britain had a Welfare State.

The last chapter discussed the development of important welfare services which were mainly concerned with mothers and children and which were mainly administered locally. However, the Welfare State became much broader in scope and application, providing the whole population with services often administered centrally. By the end of the 1940s, Britain possessed a National Health Service; Social Insurance and Public Assistance were available to all in need and the Poor Law had finally been wiped from the statute book; family allowances provided a financial income for the upkeep of all children; secondary education was open to all pupils; council house building was developing rapidly; and it was Government policy to maintain high employment levels within a planned economy. Just as important, in general the social services were no longer regarded as handouts grudgingly given to the poor after a means test, but as universal services which belonged to citizens as a right in order to ensure a decent life for all. This was the Welfare State.

The foundations of state welfare were put down in the early decades of the century. The process was accelerated during the war mainly under a Coalition Government. Thus, when a Labour

Government was returned in 1945, it was well placed to build upon and extend policies which were already in progress. Why did this acceleration occur during the war and what part did evacuation play?

Changing expectations

During the war, public attitudes and expectations of welfare altered. It started with the evacuation when isolated mothers, pregnant women, troubled children (and eventually Blitzed-out families) had to turn to the Government for help. These unfortunate people approached the Government not as paupers applying to the Poor Law but as citizens who were the victims of war. The Government soon realized that if public morale— so essential for the war effort- -were to be upheld, then help would have to come via services which were of good quality and which came as a right.

There followed, at local authority level, the rest centres, the maternity units, the welfare clinics, the day nurseries and the services to children. The expansion of welfare clinics was particularly important for they were increasingly used by middle-class women, perhaps because they too felt vulnerable and isolated with their husbands in the Forces. Thus, in the reception zones, working-class evacuee mothers and affluent country ladies could sit side by side to receive the same service. The seeds of what Titmuss called universalism—the same service for all—were taking root.

The turning point in social policy, according to the historian Paul Addison, was that desperate year of 1940 when Britain stood on the brink of defeat. Food supplies from abroad were endangered and so policies had to be developed to ensure that all were fed. Clem Attlee headed a small task force of Cabinet Ministers which planned the large-scale distribution of essential foods. The Treasury rejected it as too expensive and declared for means-tested food hand-outs. The whole Cabinet over-ruled the Treasury and the school meals and milk and the welfare food schemes took off. The decision was significant in that the power of the Treasury to consistently cut down welfare expenditure was broken. Further, as Titmuss wrote soon after the war in *Problems of Social Policy*:

> *These developments in the provision of meals and milk at school expressed something very close to a revolution in the attitude of parents, teachers and children to a scheme which, only a few years earlier, had not been regarded with much respect or sympathy. In place of a relief measure, tainted with the Poor Law, it became a social service, fused into school life, and making its own contribution to the physical nurture of the children and to their social education.*

Writing a quarter of a century later, in *The Road to 1945*, Addison agreed, stating:

> *since the whole population had to endure the rigours of participating in the war effort, the Government had to cater for the welfare of all.*

Moreover, as use of the social services widened, so higher standards were expected. Citizens who were making sacrifices for their country could not be shunted off with services done on the cheap by staff who looked down upon them. Working-class as well as middle-class families were bombed out and they expected to be treated with respect and efficiency by council staff who re-housed them or saw to the repair of their homes.

Working women could look to quality care from day nurseries because they were participating in the war effort. Residential nurseries, which before the war had been associated with the children of parents who could not cope, were opened to mothers who joined the Forces or undertook essential war work (and they included some evacuee mothers). Later they became available to the children of any servicemen and they certainly would not accept the attitudes and standards which had been associated with the residential nurseries of the Public Assistance departments. In short, the emergence of universalism led to demands for higher welfare standards and gradually these demands were extended to the health, education and housing services.

Poverty perceived

The bombing and evacuation, the need for high morale, thus paved the way for more enlightened welfare practice. In regard to local welfare services and the receipt of welfare foods, the pre-war stigma that these were just for poor people was gradually removed. None the less, as far as poor people were concerned, these services might alleviate their deprivations but they could not remove their poverty. Yet, simultaneously, evacuation was also to bring to the nation something of the extent and injustice of poverty.

The existence of poverty in pre-war Britain was not unknown. A number of academic studies had identified the low levels of living of what was still called 'the submerged tenth.' Labour party leaders, like George Lansbury in East London and his fellow Christian socialist Dr Alfred Salter in south London, continually voiced their anger that abject poverty still existed amidst much luxury. Yet the lives of poor people were often separated from those of the affluent. There was no wide-scale TV to project poverty into the living rooms of the well-to-do. The importance of evacuation was that it moved poor families into their living rooms.

Of course, not all evacuees were poor. Wealthy residents of the big cities had evacuated themselves privately. Vera Brittain, while complaining about the way working-class evacuees were treated, was sending her own children, one of whom was the future politician Shirley Williams, to the safety of America. Even within the official evacuation schemes, not all were poor. But the poor were concentrated within these schemes, not in the private ones. Evacuation was disproportionately drawn from the large industrial cities wherein were crowded low-income families. Significantly, when parents were asked by the Government to contribute to the costs of their children's evacuation, over 25 per cent received a nil-assessment—that is, they were poor.

The foster parents who received the evacuees were of varying social backgrounds. There was Mrs St Loe Strachey, OBE, JP, and her county friends with their maids, cleaners, gardeners and drivers. There were the wives of bank managers, solicitors, farmers and shop-keepers. There were also homes whose wage-earners were farm labourers, postmen, porters, shop assistants and so on. But even the working-class foster parents in the country and the county towns lived very different lives of those in the packed poverty in the inner cities. In *Evacuation in Scotland*, Boyd draws upon a survey which showed that nearly all the evacuees from Clydebank were classified as working-class. The foster homes to which they went were 59 per cent wealthy and 41 per cent working-class. But the rural working class lived in very different surroundings from the tenements of Clydebank. Evacuation was a door which opened the homes of rural, often middle-class, people to the families of the urban poor. And what they saw often shocked them.

The Commission of the Churches reported of the evacuation:

The country was undoubtedly electrified to discover the dirt, poverty and ignorance, particularly of home hygiene, that still exists in large towns.

A London teacher, evacuated to the country, wrote in her diary:

It has revealed to them (those kind people who have taken them into their homes) that life does not serve us all alike with the luxuries money can buy. They have been astounded at the poor clothes these evacuees brought away with them. They have expressed surprise at their habits and environment. Perhaps evacuation has done good in that it has revealed these conditions under which many of our children have been reared. May great improvements be the outcome of these revelations.

Even Neville Chamberlain, the Prime Minister at the time, wrote to his wife:

I never knew that such conditions existed, and I feel ashamed of having been so ignorant of my neighbours. For the rest of my life I mean to try to make amends by helping such people to live cleaner and healthier lives.

The immediate reaction of many foster parents to the poor clothing, the lack of shoes, the lice, the ill-health and the behaviour so different from their own, was one of complaint. They blamed the parents for bringing up the children so badly. Gradually, however, the enforced cheek-by-jowl existence taught them many of the strengths of poor families. In Cambridge, it was noted how the evacuee children cared for and defended each other and how almost every child said that he or she would sooner be at home with mum and dad, whatever the conditions, than in the cleanliness and advantages of Cambridge. Susan Isaacs wrote:

Among the simple and the poor where there is no wealth, no pride of status or possessions, love for the members of one's own family and joy in their bodily presence alone makes life worth living.

Grumbles about the inadequacies and flightiness of evacuated mothers turned to grudging admiration as they displayed loyalty to their absent husbands and a ferocity to care for their children even when lack of money and ill-health handicapped them. Many evacuee mothers and children possessed a solidarity and a family loyalty which was, after all, in common with the values of the host community.

To many—certainly not all—residents of the reception areas, the evacuation eventually taught them that the problems, the lack of clothing, the thinness, the different manners, even the aggressiveness of the evacuees came not from a stock of 'problem families' but from a poverty which had been imposed upon them by society. Those with evacuees from Stepney might well have discovered that 90 per cent of their homes were without baths; those with children from Glasgow that that city's infant death rate was higher than that of Tokyo; those with children who preferred chips, bread and marge might have perceived that this was the diet their parents could afford; those with youngsters who slept on the floor, that they were not used to sleeping on beds. As one child wrote, 'The country is a funny place. They never tell you you can't have no more to eat, and under the bed is wasted.'

With understanding came compassion, with compassion came a determination to take action to challenge poverty. As the social historian Arthur Marwick graphically put it in *The Home Front*:

> *Ultimately, the significance of the evacuation experience was that it brought to middle- and upper-class households a consciousness for the first time of the deplorable conditions endemic in the rookeries and warrens which still existed in Britain's great industrial cities, and so, among the articulate few, aroused a new sense of social concern. In this sense evacuation was a unique experience and one of the most significant phenomena of the war.*

Lobbying for change

Among the 'articulate few' were a number of women and women's groups. During the inter-war years, women's organizations had been gaining strength. Prominent were the following:

The National Council of Women with a membership of over 13,000, of mainly well-educated women.

The National Federation of Women's Institutes, representing 338,000 countrywomen.

The National Union of Townswomen's Guilds with 554 branches and between 10–20 members in each.

The Soroptimist Clubs representing 3,500 professional women.

The Women's Mutual Service Club with around 12,000 members, mainly working-class women.

The Women's Voluntary Service, probably the foremost women's organization, having been formed in anticipation of the war and having recruited tens of thousands of members to run services for the Home Front.

The evacuation was of direct concern to all these organizations. Some 148,000 WVS members participated in organizing the evacuation. Many of the members of the National Federation of Women's Institutes were foster parents themselves while their local Institutes were often involved in initially helping the reception of evacuees and then in arranging entertainment for evacuee children and centres for evacuee mothers. The National Council of Women gave much time to planning for post-war Britain. All the groups discussed the evacuation and over twenty of them came together in The Women's Group On Problems Arising From Evacuation. At the time, Mass Observation, in recording the work of women's organizations, noted 'how important a factor for the formulation of public opinion and the creation of civilian morale they have become.' And increasingly they tried to influence that opinion towards social reform which would benefit the kind of people they had met as evacuees. Astonishingly, the evacuation, which initially provoked a fury of middle-class complaint, went on to become a movement for helping the material lot of working-class people.

To give just two examples of how women were involved in the concerns of the evacuation and its aftermath, it is interesting to look at the influence of one individual—Lady Allen—and one organization—The Women's Group on Public Welfare. Marjory Allen has already been mentioned. A pacifist who refused to participate directly in the war effort, she gave much time to helping evacuees. She joined in the demands for increased day-care provision but was disappointed when expansion came mainly with day nurseries—run by health departments—not with nursery schools under the lead of education departments. Her case was that the latter, with their strong educational content, would be of most benefit to evacuee children in preparing them for school and later academic progress. She raised funds for demonstration projects and trebled the membership of the Nursery School Association. She displayed the skills both of gaining coverage in the press and also of developing political contacts. She persuaded Herbert Morrison, then Home Secretary, to open one of the demonstration projects. Perhaps Morrison did not need much persuasion because he later proposed marriage—which she declined. She was successful in getting the case for nursery education put into official planning for the future of British schools.

Lady Allen was a strong individualist, a team captain rather than a team player. More representative of involved women was The Women's Group On Public Welfare. This organization responded to a request from the National Federation of Women's Institutes to consider the problems being revealed by evacuation. The Group set up a committee of eight professional women who then called twenty-seven witnesses, such as health visitors, local government officials and social workers; in addition it studied reports, publications and research. Its final Report, published as the powerful *Our Towns: A Close-Up* revealed that its members had been profoundly shocked at what they found. 'The dreadful lesson of evacuation,' the Report stated, 'was the light it threw upon the home conditions of the lowest of the town dwellers.' They found that London possessed 70,000 over-crowded houses and Liverpool 11,500. The committee members were horrified at the infant mortality and child mortality rates in the cities from which the evacuees had come. They were saddened at the lack of sanitation, the density of industrial smoke, the lack of green places and play space. They established that in those towns some 22–30 per cent of children were in dire poverty. The committee acknowledged that low incomes were also found in the country but added that country families did not suffer 'the special town conditions of overcrowding, lack of open spaces, smoke and noise.'

At times, *Our Towns: A Close-Up* does refer to 'problem families', implying that within the slums there was an ineducable minority which bred trouble-makers, disease and delinquency. Yet gradually this tone is replaced by the deduction that it is not personal bad habits which create poverty but vice versa. How could families, like many of the evacuee families, keep clothes clean if, as one survey found, nearly half had recourse only to a kettle? How could children be kept clean if two-thirds of their homes had no bath? How could lice be avoided if so many lived in overcrowded conditions? The Report came to the startling conclusion that it was not the evacuees who were to blame, not the residents of the cities from where they came, no, the whole nation was to blame for allowing such deprivations. In the words of the Report, 'Now that through evacuation the depth of our social failure can be appreciated, can any measures be found which seem to hold real hope for amelioration?'

The Report then turned to concrete proposals for improving the lot of poor people. They range from suggestions of minute detail, such as the marketing of a square-toothed steel nit comb affordable by all and slot machines to sell low-priced soluble sanitary towels, to proposals of radical social reforms. Amongst the most important were the following:

Nursery education for all children for therein 'habits can be formed, health and nutrition safeguarded, and the tender mind ineradicably influenced for good'.

Education had to be vastly improved with no class size over thirty, secondary schooling available for all, and the school leaving age raised to sixteen. Most important, schools had to have able and committed teachers, refreshed by time off for new courses every seven years while 'the existence of a bar on the employment of married women teachers should be relegated to the limbo where it belongs.'

Good housing had to be promoted as one of the keys to good family life. The Report wanted not just direct provision by local authorities but also wanted private landlords, whom it called 'the spoilt child of the law', made to install baths, indoor toilets and cooking facilities in all their properties.

Better health ensured by 'a national medical service designed to lift the crushing burden of ill-health and disability which is one of the most distressing sources and symptoms of poverty.'

Poverty itself had to be tackled by children's allowances, by the abolition of low wages, and by the control of food prices. It added, 'Trade and industry must take their place as servants, not masters, of the community, recognising a duty not only economic but moral.'

The Report does contain some conservative asides, such as the assumption that working-class girls most needed an education to train them as mothers. But, overall, it is breathtakingly radical and contains both values and proposals which still have not been attained today. Perhaps its most surprising and enlightening feature is its insistence that evacuees and the poor people they represent are not some kind of inferior species, what would be called an 'underclass' today, but rather human beings who possess courage, humour, values and the 'constant greatness of the human spirit.' In short, the Report develops a high regard for poor people and ends with the noble words, 'Great and radical reforms are needed to give humanity its chance... If we believe in human dignity and human worth, we must take up the challenge of September, 1939.'

Published in 1943, *Our Towns: A Close-Up* soon sold out and quickly ran to two more printings. It received wide press coverage and was fed back into the women's organizations and country areas. In short, it influenced what had been regarded as the more conservative parts of Britain and through them put pressure on the makers of local and national policy.

It was not just the middle classes who were moved by the evacuation to agitate for a better Britain. There were also the evacuees themselves. Ben Wicks, himself an evacuee, and after studying hundreds of accounts by evacuees, concluded in *No Time To Wave Goodbye*:

> *the evacuation shattered many people's belief that authority was there to be blindly obeyed. The evacuees had suffered the humiliation of being treated like cattle as they waited to be picked out and carried away by strangers. Mothers who had received calls for help from their children had rushed to their aid and, in defiance of the Government, had brought them home again. The confidence of the working class grew. They were ready to shape the country's destiny.*

Mothers did battle with authority. Often they won new billets and they saw rest centres and welfare clinics opened for them.

More, they and their children witnessed at first-hand how the other half lived. For the first time, they went into homes that were spacious, met people who had well-paid and secure employment, lived close to children who were well-fed, well-looking and well-educated. And they began to ask why they had been sentenced to poverty in the urban slums. Moreover, the feeling grew that if their husbands were good enough to fight for the nation and if they were willing to endure the Blitz or be moved away because of it, then the same nation should be prepared to give them a fairer share of its goods. As Lucy Faithfull observed:

The evacuation scheme was a great leveller. People who had put up with awful conditions in the slums suddenly had windows opened to them. They realized what they hadn't got and they began to pressurize for better housing, for better situations, certainly they wanted something better for their children.

The evacuation did not start a revolt but some women were politicized by it and went home ready to demand a better deal for their families and resolved to vote for politicians who would make these demands a reality.

Not least, the evacuation, along with the bombing, brought about some unity between different sections of the community. True, some of the residents in the reception areas were initially both horrified at and angry with the evacuees. True, the evacuees often found their hosts to be critical and patronising. Yet the passage of time and the presence of a common enemy did bring together different classes. *Wartime Women* records the Mass Observation diary of Mrs Trowbridge, a middle-aged housewife with a prosperous husband, a son about to go to Oxford, and the holder of strong anti-socialist convictions. Active in the University Women's Federation, she found herself at the beginning of the war drawn into its efforts on behalf of refugees from Europe. She then gave lodgings to an ordinary soldier. Before long she was involved in persuading the authorities to set up a nursery for evacuee children. Then she was battling to ensure that the children and their mothers should get free milk. In a way that would not have been possible before the war she was at one with the evacuees. The perceptive priest, Father Groser, wrote in *Politics and Persons* that the war and evacuation

> *brought about something that Marx never thought posssible.*
> *By itself the working-class movement can never carry through a*
> *peaceful revolution on the scale which is demanded, in a*
> *country where a large middle class exists, without the active*
> *help of that class. Whereas before the war on the whole that*
> *middle class was fearful of radical changes and of working-*
> *class aims, the war had brought a new understanding and a*
> *desire for common action.*

The evacuation not only opened the eyes of many middle-class residents of the more prosperous parts of Britain to the conditions of the home cities of the evacuees, it also forged something of a bond between them. As Professor Titmuss, who lived through the war and studied its impact for the Government, concluded, 'the evacuation of mothers and children and the bombing of homes during 1939–40, stimulated enquiry and proposals for reform long before victory was even thought possible.'

Not just the evacuation

A fire for social change was lit during the war. But evacuation was only one of its flames and others must be mentioned. The war-time conditions created both a greater experience of equality and a desire for more equality across a wide range of citizens. The ration book was a great leveller. The weekly ration in 1941 of eight ounces of meat, one ounce of cheese, four ounces of bacon or ham, eight ounces of fats and two ounces of jam, applied to all. For the higher income groups it meant a reduction in food intake but for the poor and unemployed it could mean an improved diet.

Moreover, the lot of the latter improved in another way. The war demanded manpower (and woman power) at home as well as in the Forces abroad. Unem-ployment was virtually abolished while wage packets increased because of overtime. Incomes from wages rose by 18 per cent during 1938–47, while those from salaries fell by 21 per cent and profits from property fell by 15 per cent. Those who gained did not want the clock put back. As far as rationing was concerned, a poll in 1942 came up with the surprising result that it was popular and that many people wanted it continued after the war.

Greater equality seemed right for a nation in a war which involved all its citizens. Consequently, some anger was expressed at the minority who did obtain more. Food coupons were not required in restaurants where the rich could still buy some luxuries such as salmon. One demonstration even invaded the Savoy hotel where the wealthy diners were saved by the advent of an air raid. Again, resentment was expressed towards the owners of posh cars who somehow obtained petrol while the owners of small vehicles could not get enough to drive to work. Much more than before the war, the feeling was rife that the rich should be deprived of some of their goods for the sake of those who had little.

The war on the home front also meant a huge participation in service. In contrast to the First World War where, for Britain, nearly all the action was abroad, the Second World War involved thousands of men and women in active service at home. Over 1,500,000 men joined the Home Guard and spent much of their time in rescue work following air raids. The air raid wardens, the stretcher parties, the emergency ambulance service, the WVS, involved thousands, mainly as volunteers. Even many of the fire fighters were auxiliaries. Many were ordinary, working-class citizens who had not previously participated in official civic organizations. Father John Groser, up to his neck in the war-time volunteer movements, noted the effect on previously unemployed people:

> *The coming of the war . . . lifted the working class at once out of that awful trough of despair and made its members feel that they were persons again, with a real part to play in life.*

Moreover, as members of vital organizations, these citizens, both working- and middle-class, perceived that they could play a part in shaping the future. In a famous war-time passage, J.B. Priestley noted that the war was 'a citizen's war' and that its members were

*a new type, what might be called the organized militant
citizen. And the whole circumstances of their war-time life
favour a sharply democratic outlook. Men and women with a
gift for leadership now turn up in unexpected places. The new
ordeals blast away the old shams. Britain, which in the years
immediately before this war was rapidly losing such
democratic virtues as it possessed, is now being bombed and
burned into democracy.*

The active participation of civilians did not mean that the armed forces were in a different mood about social reform. Far from it. For long periods, they were training and waiting. To break the monotony, discussion groups and lectures were organized and they revealed a strong desire for better social services and a more equal Britain. The radicalism alarmed some top brass officers but it was considered that to then stop the debate would make matters worse. The feelings of rank and file troops found immediate expression concerning the way their families were treated. When some wives of servicemen became ill or could not cope, their children were sometimes received into the care of Public Assistance institutions. Their husbands, eventually backed by officers, protested that they should not go into Poor Law bodies but into the day nurseries or residential nurseries being provided to help evacuees. The Ministry of Health had to agree. Again, soldiers, sailors and airmen voiced concern about home housing conditions, especially when their families were re-housed after bombing. There was a desire for change, almost a militancy, within the forces quite different from the conservatism of their fathers who had fought, and died, in the trenches, some twenty odd years before. So obvious was the new spirit that in early 1943 a number of Tory army officers, including Peter Thorneycroft, Quentin Hogg and Lord Hinchingbroke, left the forces to return to politics in order to impress the Conservative party that it had to become more reformist in line with the views of the troops.

In March 1943, the Labour MP Emmanuel Shinwell wrote that 'the time is now ripe for the consideration of our future pattern of living; only the ignorant will assert that there is not a greater public desire for radical social change than ever before in our long history.' In fact, Labour MPs, as members of the Coalition Government, could not campaign for radical change on party political lines. Such limitations did not apply to trade unions. The restoration of full employment and the demand for skilled labour had resulted in trade union membership rising steeply to over 8,000,000. Their new strength was used to win wage rises but they also made the case for a more socialist Britain. In addition, they pointed out the weaknesses of the social services. In 1941, the Trade Unions Congress sent a deputation to the Minister of Health, Malcolm MacDonald, to urge reform of the National Insurance system and of the organization of hospitals. The seeds of the Beveridge Report were being planted.

Women's movements, evacuees, the citizens' armies, the troops, the trade unions, all contained individuals and groups which were pressing for social reforms. They were joined by a powerful voice from an unexpected quarter—the Christian church.

Throughout the earlier part of the century, the church had contained radical vicars and organizations committed to social justice such as the Christian Social Union and the Church Socialist League. Richard Tawney was the great exponent of Christian socialism and George Lansbury one of its foremost practitioners. Yet they had been minority voices often over-ruled by more conservative elements so that the Church of England still retained the image of 'the Tory party at prayer'. Yet, during the war, leading church figures added their weight to the call for a fairer and more equal Britain.

The Roman Catholic Cardinal Hinsley of Westminster had founded The Sword of the Spirit as a crusade 'for the restoration of a Christian order of justice and peace'. Non-conformist churches were running Religion and Life Weeks to discuss social issues. The church leaders came together. On 21 December 1940 Cardinal Hinsley, the Archbishop of Canterbury Cosmo Lang, the Archbishop of York William Temple, and the Moderator of the Free Church Federal Council the Rev Walter Armstrong had a letter published in *The Times* which made a considerable impact. After calling for international peace, it proposed five aims for all nations as follows:

1. *Extreme inequality in wealth and possessions should be abolished.*

2. *Every child, regardless of race or class, should have equal opportunities of education suitable for the development of his peculiar capacities.*

3. *The family as a social unit must be safeguarded.*

4. *The sense of a Divine vocation must be restored to man's daily work.*

5. *The resources of the earth should be used as God's gift to the whole human race, and used with due consideration for the needs of the present and future generations.*

The church, which numerically had been in decline, was given a new hearing on radio and in newspapers and journals. What accounts for this? One reason was that the war, with its losses abroad and the Blitz at home, provoked a fear which made more people receptive to the concept of a protecting God. A popular hymn adapted to the time was:

God is our refuge, be not afraid,
He will be with you all through the raid.

Another reason was that to many the rise of fascism could only be explained by the existence of evil. And if evil existed it followed that so should the power of good, namely God. *The New Statesman* ran a series of articles by well-known figures who increasingly proclaimed the truth of Christianity. Not least, evacuation again had an influence. The involvement of Christians in serving evacuees acted as a witness for the church. But further, the condition of the evacuees convinced church bodies that Christians must battle for a better Britain. The Commission of Churches stated in 1941:

*The truth is that so long as the wretched material and moral
conditions which evacuation has disclosed are allowed to
disfigure our land it cannot be claimed that we are defending
Christian civilisation. The church must be roused to a fresh
struggle upon two related fronts—the fight for spiritual
renewal and the fight for social regeneration ... It is the war
from which there is no discharge for the followers of Christ.*

The stage was ready for a Christian spokesperson and it came in
the person of William Temple, who was to become Archbishop of
Canterbury in 1942. Born in 1881, the son of a bishop, Temple
went to Rugby School and Balliol College, Oxford. On entering the
church, such a privileged background seemed to guarantee him
high ecclesiastical office. His experiences were widened by time
spent at university settlements in the East End of London.
Between 1918–27, he was a member of the Labour party and his
sympathies were clearly with working-class people. He became
Bishop of Manchester and then Archbishop of York. At York, he
established himself as an accomplished speaker and writer and in
1940 he made six broadcasts which were well received and
immediately published in journals. Temple, sensing an audience
for what he was saying, went quickly to work and in December
1940 published *The Hope of a New World*.

Temple regarded Britain as Christian in its cultural heritage and
in the adherence of many of its citizens to the church. He
considered that two factors were required to make it more
Christian. One was that there should be a larger body of people
who 'have found the redeeming power of what is in Christ.' Thus
Temple supported evangelistic efforts to bring people into a
relationship with God. The other was that the country had to be
ordered according to Christian principles. He did not see himself
as a political leader and did not want the church identified with any
one political party. Rather, it was the church's duty both to remind
the State that it was responsible to God and to provide a theological
foundation for all parties.

What was this foundation? In *The Hope of a New World*,
Temple starts with the premise that God is central to all aspects

of life and that religion is not simply a private matter between an individual and God. Next, he argued that all people are created by God, are of unique value to him, and therefore all have a claim to the resources and the responsibilities of the world. Freedom he saw not as doing as one pleased but 'freedom to do what I ought and to fulfil God's purposes for me'. And God's purposes were that all people should both enjoy the goodness of the earth and contribute to ensuring that others had their share.

Unfortunately, Temple continued, the presence of sin led to policies and structures which nullified freedom for some. These structures might be the distribution of land and property into the hands of the few whereas the Bible clearly taught that they should be dispersed among the many. They might be the profit motive becoming so dominating that market forces led to some citizens not even having enough to meet their basic needs. It followed that, in order to put Christian principles into practice, society, through its elected bodies, had a duty both to limit the accumulation of wealth by elites and also to counter poverty.

Temple was writing in 1940 when the war had pushed the Government into extending state control over some of the major means of economic production and distribution for the good of the nation. Its proper action, Temple reasoned, constituted a rightful precedent so that 'the claims over private enterprise, established for war-time purposes, shall be retained when peace returns.' He advocated also the introduction of family allowances to alleviate poverty. More radically, he wanted the State to take over the Bank of England so that the Government, not private enterprise, controlled the issue of money and credit. Temple made clear that he was not in favour of wholesale State ownership and certainly did not want the abolition of private enterprise but that he did believe that, in a Christian community, the State had to intervene to ensure social justice.

The Hope of a New World appeared shortly before a major conference at Malvern College in January 1941. Organized by the Industrial Christian Fellowship, it was chaired by Temple and its participants included fifteen bishops, 400 clergy and notable figures such as Dorothy Sayers, T.S. Eliot and Sir Richard Acland MP. Acland wanted the conference to express complete opposition to private property by declaring that common ownership was fundamental to Christian principles. Temple skilfully drew together what he called the 'common mind' of the conference in a statement which said that individual salvation was a spiritual process but that Christians then had to work out their beliefs in the running of a society in which private ownership 'might' be a stumbling block to social progress. There followed a number of recommendations for action by the Government. T.S. Eliot and a few others dissociated themselves from the statement but it carried sufficient weight to win much publicity outside. The summary of the proceedings went into two pamphlets which sold over a million copies. Temple then drew upon the conference to publish *Christianity and the Social Order* which sold 139,000 copies.

By this time, Temple was Archbishop of Canterbury. When Archbishop Cosmo Lang retired, some Conservative MPs had expressed opposition to Temple whose abilities and position within the church marked him as the obvious successor. But the only other serious candidate was Bishop Bell of Chichester who had annoyed Conservatives even more by his opposition to RAF night bombing of civilian targets in Europe. So in February 1942, aged sixty-one, Temple proceeded to Canterbury.

It was a popular choice and not only within the church. On leaving office, Cosmo Lang had complained that it was going to be difficult for him to cope on his slender means. *The Daily Mirror* pointed out that his slender means was an annual pension of fifteen hundred pounds. Temple was regarded as being much more in touch with ordinary people. He had the ability of communicating in everyday language and became a frequent broadcaster. In the autumn of 1942, he organized a series of public meetings in London and other cities which were sold out two months before their date. Temple repeated his gospel that individuals needed a personal relationship with God and that this relationship then had to be expressed in service to neighbours, which might entail social reforms for their benefit. In particular, he argued that the State should take over all monopolies in essential industries to ensure that they were run for the common good. He provoked some hostility, with a number of Conservative figures protesting that the church should not meddle in politics. Randolph Churchill rose in the Commons to remark sarcastically that it might be considered 'very bad taste for a mere politician to make a speech on a political subject.' Yet Temple, unlike Randolph Churchill, was increasingly seen as one who spoke for a much wider following than the church. Then suddenly, in September 1944, he died. The public reaction to his death was widespread and genuine. It was akin to that for the politician John Smith in 1994 and for similar reasons. He was regarded as a decent, honest, Christian man whose life had been devoted to others more than to himself.

The Beveridge Report

The voice of the church added to the pressure for social reform which the Government found difficult to resist. The Coalition Government had already implemented massive state planning as part of the war effort. In 1940, John Maynard Keynes, the economist who stood for greater government control of the economy, joined the Treasury. Obviously, Labour members of the Government welcomed these developments which they saw as both socialist in nature and also pleasing to the electorate. The Conservatives were divided. A number of their MPs considered that concessions would have to be be made to the growing demands and that they had best come under a Government headed by Winston Churchill. They were not unchallenged and other Conservative members sided with right-wing pressure groups such as Aims of Industry, formed in 1942 to stop the slide away from free enterprise, and the National League of Freedom, which saw state intervention as a limitation of the freedom of private business people to operate as they wished. Churchill wavered between the two but eventually agreed that some kind of enquiry would be in order.

Following the TUC's approaches over the inadequacies of the National Insurance system, the Government thus agreed to set up a review. The Minister of Labour, Ernie Bevin, wanted to be rid of one of his advisors, the distinguished Sir William Beveridge, who was therefore appointed its chairperson. Beveridge perceived that he was being shunted aside but, as his wife Janet wrote in her biography of him, he saw it as 'a heaven-sent opportunity ... to bring to a head at last in a single comprehensive scheme the principles of his work on social security which had been developing and maturing in his continuous preoccupation with the problems over a period of nearly forty years.'

The one-man report was published in 1942 as the *Report on Social Insurance and Allied Services*. In order to attack the five giants of 'Want, Disease, Ignorance, Squalor and Idleness', it proposed a comprehensive state insurance scheme, with individuals and employers compelled to make weekly contributions, which would pay out benefits to meet needs associated with unemployment, disability and illness, retirement, widowhood, and other associated needs such as funeral expenses. Both the payments in and the benefits out were to be at a flat rate and, most importantly, would be given as a right, not as the result of a means test. Beveridge added that his scheme was based on the assumption that the Government would also be introducing a National Health Service and family allowances and would be maintaining full employment. Thus at the time, when Germany was invading Russia and Japan was sinking the American fleet in Pearl Harbour, Beveridge was writing the blueprint of a Welfare State with a national minimum income for all, quite independent of the Poor Law.

The publication of the Beveridge Report met furious opposition from the Federation of British Industries. *The Daily Telegraph* condemned it as state socialism. But generally it was welcomed with an enthusiastic response. The Report, along with its official summary, sold over 635,000 copies. Its appeal was in the simplicity of its proposals, for they abolished the complicated and varying pre-war schemes and united them into one weekly contribution along with the same benefits for all. It thus fitted the mood of the country which was both to abolish poverty and to promote greater equality. Accordingly, a Gallup poll found that the vast majority of the population wanted the Report put into operation.

The public reaction was a confirmation that attitudes had changed within Britain. As early as July 1940, *The Times*, usually considered the organ of the establishment, was writing of the future in these words:

If we speak of democracy, we do not mean a democracy which maintains the right to vote but forgets the right to work and the right to live. If we speak of freedom, we do not mean a rugged individualism which excludes social organization and economic planning. If we speak of equality we do not mean a political equality nullified by social and economic privilege.

The circulation of *The Daily Mirror*, the most anti-Tory paper, jumped from 1,750,000 in 1939 to 3,000,000 in 1946. The change must not be exaggerated. Overall, the circulation of right-wing daily papers still outstripped that of left-wing ones. None the less, a Mass Observation poll in 1942 estimated that two out of five people had changed their political outlook since the war started and there was little doubt that the shift was towards a desire for a vast extension of state welfare and public ownership. All this occurred while party political campaigning was in an uneasy truce. The changes were mainly due to the experiences and movements described in this chapter, attributable among other things to the Blitz and the evacuation.

Action

The public desire for social reform was not just seen in the enthusiastic response to the Beveridge Report. Other reports and collective action went on all through the war. Chamberlain's War Cabinet, which was essentially a Conservative administration, had soon acknowledged that the British health system was ill-equipped to deal with large-scale bombing. It organized an Emergency Hospital Service which effectively brought the nation's hospitals under Government direction and so ensured that all were supplied with essential medical equipment. Later, the Government ensured free treatment for war casualties, then for evacuees and then for all. A national blood transfusion service was set up. The replacement of the previously fragmented hospital service by a unified one allowed for a far better distribution of medical personnel and resources. The desirability of retaining such a service after the war was high on the political agenda. In 1941 the Coalition Government pledged itself to a national hospital service after the war and by 1942 it was planning a national service of general medical practitioners.

Early in 1944, when the end of the war was in sight, the Government issued a White Paper, *A National Health Service*. It proposed free, good quality hospital and general practitioner services for all. It was to be centrally organized and financed by taxation and would include dental and optical care. The panels, the insurance schemes, the means tests, would be abolished, so giving a universal service to all.

The White Paper had its critics. *The Ilford Recorder* generally praised the proposals but considered that they did not go far enough. It pointed out that the provision to allow medical practitioners and voluntary hospitals to choose to stay out of the scheme could lead to a two-tier system with the wealthy again getting preferential treatment. The leaders of the British Medical Association put up opposition on the grounds that it would lead to bureaucracy controlling medicine. Generally, however, the proposals won widespread support. This even extended to most doctors for, as Angus Calder makes clear, the leadership of the BMA was dominated by 'wealthy GPs from the suburbs and the spas' whereas 'the struggling doctors in working-class areas, ill-paid salaried men in the public hospitals, and young doctors in the armed forces' were mostly for the proposals. The war had brought about something approaching a National Health Service and few wanted to go back to the cumbersome and unequal system of 1939.

In that year of 1939, some 1,250,000 people had been unemployed. Once the war commenced, their numbers fell rapidly not only because of conscription but also because the Government took on the training and distribution of civilian workers in order to maximize industrial production. Politicians from all parties acknowledged the advantages of having Government rather than the private market in charge of employment. In 1944, the Government published a White Paper on employment policy which indicated that, after the war, the state would still need to intervene in the economy in order to maintain high employment.

If employment became an acceptable sphere of Government action then how much more was education. The evacuation showed up the differences between town and country schools, revealed the poor conditions of many urban schools, and lay bare the low attainment levels of many evacuees. As Angus Calder put it, 'Evacuation had made education a burning political issue.' As Susan Lawrence argued, the war not only showed the deficiencies of the education system, it also presented the opportunity for progress.

R.A. Butler became President of the Board of Education in the midst of this controversy in 1941. A Conservative, he believed that Britain required a more educated population and he perceived that the current system was not supplying it. He joined forces with Labour's James Chuter-Ede, who had a background in teaching, to formulate and then pass the Education Act 1944. The Act is best known for ensuring free secondary education for all within a proposed tripartite system of secondary modern, technical and grammar schools. The school leaving age was to be raised to fifteen in 1945 (later postponed to 1947). An act of religious worship of a nondenominational kind was made compulsory for all state schools. Perhaps most important, a Ministry of Education was set up with greater powers to impose educational policy over the disparate local authorities, who were to remain responsible for running the schools.

Finally, one of the last enactments of the Coalition Government was one of its most important. The Family Allowances Act 1945 gave every family five shillings a week for second and subsequent children under school leaving age. By providing a secure income, given to all families as a right and not subject to a means test, and related to family size, it provided one of the most significant pieces of anti-poverty legislation in the twentieth century. Along with the other enactments and proposals outlined in this section, it demonstrates how the war—including the evacuation—had pushed the Government—and a Coalition Government, not a Labour one—into collective action because such was in the best interests of the nation. Backed by a war-time public mood that also wanted reform, the government extended state welfare in ways which could not possibly have been anticipated before the war.

The Welfare State

Once the war ended, a general election took place. It resulted in a Labour victory with Labour gaining 393 seats, Conservatives 213, and Liberals 12. The defeat of the magnificent war leader, Winston Churchill, came as a surprise to some. The explanation is that he was not in tune with the changing attitudes and wishes of the British people. As the historian, Paul Addison, put it, 'the most remarkable feature of the war was the way in which the ideal of a more egalitarian society gained momentum and support.' Churchill had been lukewarm in his support of the Beveridge Report. He had no clear strategy for the establishment of a Welfare State which was wanted by many. Churchill was once dismayed to find that Ernie Bevin cleaned his own shoes and amazed when he declined the offer of a batman. This small incident illustrates what many people thought, that Churchill did not appreciate how ordinary people lived and did not understand how they thought. By contrast, the Labour Party was clearly identified with the reforms that had occurred and offered a manifesto to extend them. Moreover, the war-time coalition had given ministerial experience to their politicians, particularly Clem Attlee, Ernie Bevin, Herbert Morrison, Hugh Dalton and Tom Johnston. They thus constituted a creditable alternative Government in a way which they did not in 1939.

The new Government soon set about fulfilling its promise to install a Welfare State. In 1946 the National Insurance Act and the National Health Service Act were passed, 1947 included the Town and Country Planning Act, and in 1948 the National Assistance Act with its memorable words, 'The existing Poor Law shall cease to have effect.' A housing drive led to the building of 1,000,000 houses as well as creating much employment. In addition to these specifically welfare enactments, there were also the nationalization of the Bank of England (which would have pleased Temple), and the taking into public ownership of coal, electricity, gas, the railways and the iron and steel industry. Clem Attlee later explained in his autobiography that the Labour Party's objective was 'the creation of a society based on social justice, and, in our view, this could only be attained by bringing under public ownership and control the main factors in the economic system.'

At the time, these reforms were hailed or hated as extensive. Some rejoiced in the abolition of the Poor Law and the establishment of minimum standards. Others bemoaned that Britain was 'halfway to Moscow'. In later years, however, some academics played down the achievements. It was pointed out that capitalism still remained. Macnicol argued that a minority of consultants still wielded the power within the health service and that the new social security rates were set too low. On the education front, Labour was attacked for accepting the tripartite division of secondary education and for leaving private schools in existence.

There is force in these arguments. Certainly Britain had not become a completely socialist society by the end of the Attlee administration. The distribution of capital was such that much economic power remained with a minority of the population. Entry to the higher posts of the civil service, the professions and the media was still biased towards those with a public school or Oxbridge education. The belief that poverty was abolished proved false. In 1950, the social investigator, Seebohm Rowntree, repeated his famous survey of York and found that only 1.66 per cent of the population was in poverty compared with 17.7 per cent in 1936. But, two events overtook this finding. One was inflation which meant that the value of wages and the price of goods rose much more rapidly than that of state benefits. The other was that poverty became defined in relative terms, that is, it was seen not just as a lack of money to cover essential needs but as an unacceptable difference from the standards enjoyed by the majority of the population. Thus the famous study by Brian Abel-Smith and Peter Townsend argued that in the 1950s some 7 per cent of the population were in poverty.

Despite these objections, I believe that profound changes did occur in the 1940s. In 1939, the Poor Law was still in existence while entitlement to unemployment and insurance benefits was patchy in coverage and temporary in duration: by the late 1940s, the Poor Law had been finally buried and entitlement to state benefits, including old age pensions, extended across the nation. In 1939, the prospect of family allowances was unlikely: by 1945 they were in place. In 1939, only 14 per cent of children proceeded to secondary education and funding of state schools was parsimonious at best: a decade later all children had secondary education while finance was no longer a barrier to working-class children going to grammar schools or higher education. In 1939, the health service was a fragmented muddle with access to medical practitioners difficult for many low-income women and children and with hospitals distributed in no logical way: by the late 1940s, the National Health Service was in place with access to services depending on need, not ability to pay. In 1939, economic policy was dominated by private interests with state intervention to control unemployment kept to a minimum: by the 1940s, the Government accepted a duty to maintain high employment. In 1939, state welfare was frugal and seen as a social ambulance for the poorest: by the end of the 1940s it was seen as a means of benefiting all. Arthur Marwick, who rates with Titmuss as the major social historian of the war years, writes in *The Home Front*:

> *Yet if we compare the attitudes towards social questions and towards class rampant in the 1930s with those of the late 1940s, we can immediately see that much has changed. The keynote of the new Welfare State legislation was 'universalism'—that is to say that there should not be a first-class service for those who paid and second-class service for those who did not.*

Not least, in 1939, the Conservative Party was strongly opposed to major extensions of state welfare: by the 1940s, many of its members had come to what was called a 'consensus' with Labour over the Welfare State. This meant, that when the Conservatives did succeed to power, the Welfare State was not immediately dismantled.

War does not necessarily lead to massive social reform. In the election following the First World War, Labour fared badly and Lloyd George's post-war Government certainly did not provide 'homes fit for heroes'. The Second World War was different for Britain. It was fought on the home front as well as abroad. What ensued should not be romanticized: it was not about cheerful cockneys proving that they could take it while humming Vera Lynn songs. War at home was cruel, destructive and deadly. Families were split assunder by conscription and evacuation. The Blitz was terrifying. The bombs destroyed 200,000 houses, rendered another 250,000 unusable, severely damaged a fifth of all schools and flattened numerous factories and public buildings. Above all, over 60,000 people were killed and some 86,000 were seriously injured by the bombs.

The immediate outcome of the terror and destruction was partly to worsen social provision. The housing shortage became more intense during the war. The bombing of school buildings and the absence of young teachers made for more crowded classrooms. None the less, welfare services were generally extended during the war and established within the framework of a Welfare State after it. These reforms might have come eventually even without the events of 1939–45 but there is no doubt that they hastened it. For in 1939 the Labour Party had no prospects of winning an election while the Chamberlain administration was still pursuing policies of retrenchment. The fact is that war on the home front led to conditions which revealed social need, to Government responses which extended social services, and to attitudes which demanded more reform. Evacuation was just one factor amongst a number which led to these developments. But it was an important factor. The evacuation of hundreds of thousands of children and mothers necessitated the enlargement of welfare services and in ways which did not treat them as paupers. Simultaneously, evacuation also became a screen on to which the poverty of urban Britain was projected for a middle-class audience. It caused *The Economist* to state in May 1943 that evacuation was 'the most important subject in the social history of the war because it revealed to the whole people the black spots in its social life.' The result was to unite some sections of the middle and working classes in a campaign both for the alleviation of poverty and for welfare services acceptable to all. As A.J.P. Taylor explained, 'The *Luftwaffe* was a powerful missionary for the Welfare State', for their bombs led to evacuation and evacuation to 'a social revolution.'

7 Warfare to child care

One piece of post-war legislation has been strangely neglected by writers. The Children Act 1948 is mentioned neither by Clem Attlee in his autobiography nor by historian Kenneth Morgan in his well-received *The People's Peace: British History 1945–89*. Yet the Act transformed the care of deprived children. It removed the spirit of the Poor Law legislation, which still required the authorities 'to set to work' destitute children, and replaced it with an Act which contains, as the children's historian Jean Heywood put it, 'a clause, perhaps unmatched for its humanity in all our legislation', namely that in future local authorities would have a duty towards a child in their care 'to exercise their powers with respect to him so as to further his best interests, and to afford him opportunity for the proper development of his character and abilities.'

The Children Act is sometimes attributed to Lady Allen. Brian Rodgers writes, 'It arose from a letter written by Lady Allen of Hurtwood to *The Times* asking that the lot of the "homeless" child be examined.' In fact, the genesis of the legislation went far beyond one woman. Like much other social legislation of that period, its shape and stimulus came from the experiences of the war in general and evacuation in particular. But for this to be understood something must be said about the state of child care in 1939.

Pre-war children's services

Before 1939, and stretching back to medieval times, the care of children with no parents, or parents unable to care for them, had been shared between voluntary bodies and the State. Amongst the voluntary bodies, child care societies began to take over from the church during the eighteenth and nineteenth centuries. Dr Barnardo's, the National Children's Home and Orphanage, the Waifs and Strays Society, Muller's Homes, Quarrier's Homes and many more were founded, often in reaction to the inhumanities of the Poor Law, and expanded rapidly. In 1907, Dr Barnardo's cared for 11,277 children. By the 1930s, however, the pioneering zeal of the great voluntaries had departed. There were minor developments with a growing interest in adoption and in giving small grants to unmarried mothers to enable them to cope at home. Generally, however, they continued to concentrate on residential care which far out-weighed any interest in fostering. Moreover, many of the homes remained large—there were over 1,000 children at the Barnardo Village Homes in Ilford—and the children were often educated on site until they were discharged unready for the world outside. It was left to smaller homes, like the Children's Home and Mission in Woodford, to show that children could be integrated into local schools and could be helped to find employment.

The State's responsibility for homeless and destitute children had long been exercised through the Poor Law. During the nineteenth century, some Poor Law unions (groups of Poor Law institutions) attempted to remove children from the workhouses and developed enormous 'barrack' schools. Later, some initiated groups of cottage homes which were smaller in size but still cut off from main-stream life. It was the Poor Law which gave an impetus to the boarding-out or fostering of its children although their schemes were criticized for a lack of supervision and low quality foster homes. But, over all, most children with no families able to look after them remained in institutions where they had little contact with their parents.

Probably the most enlightened child care thinking in the 1920s and 30s was in the field of delinquency. Reform schools (later approved schools) had started in the nineteenth century as an alternative to sending juveniles to prison. The Children Act of 1908 established juvenile courts and remand homes. The institutions for offenders were frequently large, regimented and harsh yet some liberal influences were at hand. In 1922, the Home Office founded its Children's Branch where its staff contained some progressive thinkers. They advocated probation as an alternative to detention and, within the institutions, called—often in vain—for more relaxed atmospheres and greater contact with parents in order to facilitate the offenders' eventual return home. The Children and Young Persons Act of 1933 placed a duty upon local authority education departments to bring delinquent and neglected children to court and to be responsible for them after committal. Education departments then had to develop their own residential establishments along with fostering, as well as finding staff for these functions. As some departments were listening to the advice of the growing influence of psychologists, a number of their children's homes did put an emphasis on care and treatment rather than control and punish-ment. Further, a minority of local authorities began to steer their destitute children away from the Public Assistance Departments and towards the education ones.

Despite these progressive features, the child care scene was still bleak in 1939. The majority of pauper children, swollen in numbers by the poverty of the 1930s, remained in the care of the Poor Law regimes and the voluntary societies. Both of these organizations still relied heavily on institutional care with little heed given to ideas of preventing children having to leave their natural parents, of maintaining their emotional links with them, or of working to restore them home. New organizational developments had occurred but these made for a fragmented and confusing system. At Government level, the Home Office, the Ministry of Health and the Board of Education all had responsibility for some deprived children while even the Ministry of Pensions still had duties towards children whose parents had received pensions following the First World War. At local government level, the Public Assistance Departments and Education Departments had con-siderable numbers in their care while Health Departments also looked after some destitute children in long-term hospitals. In addition, the child care voluntary societies still cared for many thousands. The child care world lacked national leaders of the standing of Barnardo in the previous century: it lacked a significant occupation associated with deprived children for social work was still in its infancy with few trained field workers while there was no recognized training for residential staff outside the in-house courses provided by Dr Barnardo's and the National Children's Home and Orphanage: not least, child care lacked public attention for the subject of children separated from their own parents was not a major issue. But then came the evacuation.

Methods of care

The advent of large-scale evacuation from 1939 onwards gave rise to debates and attention to the best methods of looking after children who had to be away from their parents. One unexpected growth was that of residential nurseries. Prior to the war, residential nurseries for young children had mainly been confined to voluntary bodies and Public Assistance Departments where they served as an initial home for destitute and homeless children before they passed on to a children's home at the age of five. At the outbreak of war, the London County Council evacuated some of its day nurseries and nursery schools as whole units where the children would live together. Overnight they became residential nurseries. Simultaneously, the war created a need for temporary residential care for small children. For instance, mothers (whose husbands were in the forces) might fall ill or go into maternity units and hence placements were required for their children: sometimes these mothers were already evacuated while others were still in the danger zones. As the war progressed, more mothers undertook war jobs with long hours, night duties and which sometimes involved being moved around the country: their children also required care.

Where should these children go? The Public Assistance Departments were not willing to open their residential nurseries to children whose parents were not destitute. Not that that worried the parents because they were not happy to let their children go into Poor Law institutions. Those run by the voluntary societies had a better reputation for they tended to attract more staff with qualifications in nursing, nursery nursing or teaching, and their accommodation was usually superior. With demands being made for more residential nurseries, the voluntary sector responded with enthusiasm. The WVS led the way but was not experienced in child care matters. Their appeal to the established societies was heard by W.R. Vaughan, the General Secretary of the Waifs and Strays Society. He immediately promised that his society would provide places for fifty evacuees needing residential care although, as John Stroud describes in his history of the Waifs and Strays, *13 Penny Stamps*, he had no idea how it would be done. In fact, by miracles of improvisation and staff recruitment, his society eventually opened one hundred war-time nurseries.

As ever, the problem was cash. At the start of the war, money flowed across the Atlantic with the American Red Cross willing to support the voluntary bodies. That source diminished when the USA entered the war, but by then the Ministry of Health had convinced the Treasury that nurseries were a part of the war effort and it was able to finance expansion. By 1942, 13,000 extra residential nursery places were in operation. Most were located in or near London where the effects of the bombing were greatest. In 1940, an analysis of applications to the London residential nurseries revealed that 47 per cent came as the result of air raids with families being left homeless, 21 per cent from parents admitted to hospital, 12 per cent for other health reasons, 15 per cent because parents had to work, and 7 per cent for other reasons. As the war continued, so the number of air raid applications diminished while those for work reasons increased.

The growth of residential nurseries, combined with their usage by a wider section of the population led to a much greater interest in their methods, usage and effects. A famous study was made of a Hampstead nursery by Dorothy Burlingham and Anna Freud (daughter of the psycho-analyst). They studied the ways small children coped with facing air raids and separation from their parents.

One of their main conclusions was that separation should be done very gradually in order to give the children time to build up relationships with new adults. This advice flew in the face of conventional child care wisdom that it was easiest if children and parents made a sudden, clean, break.

The residential expansion was not just for small children. As already explained, the needs of some older evacuee children led to the setting up of hostels or homes for them. The hostels in Cambridge, Huntingdonshire, Peebleshire and Glasgow became well known. The hostels in Oxfordshire had the advantage of the services of consultant psychiatrist Donald Winnicott, who often wrote and broadcast about his work, and the psychiatric social worker, Clare Britton, who later married Winnicott. The Winnicotts saw several hundred evacuee children and scores of staff in the hostels and they used this experience to develop views which were to be influential in the development of residential care. Thus Winnicott concluded that the aim of a hostel or home was 'to reproduce as nearly as possible a home environment for each child in it. This means first of all the provision of positive things: a building, food, clothing, human love and understanding: a timetable, schooling: apparatus and ideas leading to rich play and constructive work. The hostel also provides substitute parents and other human relationships.' This aim could be achieved only by high quality, stable staff. Winnicott favoured the employment of married wardens who provided emotional support for each other but this had to be backed by more objective support from outside from social workers and psychiatrists.

The numbers of residential nurseries and hostels declined as the evacuees went home. But Winnicott insisted that the lessons learned were still applicable to residential care because their problems had stemmed less from their experiences as evacuees and more from their unsatisfying relationships with their parents. Certainly, the evacuation had pushed residential care much more into the limelight with the following benefits:

the techniques of running establishments became matters of study with, for instance, attention given to just how small children should be introduced into a nursery or what kind of sanctions staff could apply to aggressive older children

the role of different establishments was clarified. Residential nurseries were seen as having a temporary role to look after children for short periods while parents sorted out their affairs; hostels were regarded as having a longer-term role in providing a home environment for older children with severe difficulties

the importance of good staff who possessed maturity, experience and, preferably, training, was re-iterated

central government moved towards accepting greater responsibilities for over-seeing residential work and promoting training.

The expansion of residential care following the evacuation brought it particularly to the notice of what might be called the professional audience, to people involved in welfare, to Government officials, to psychiatric staff, to those organizing the evacuation. Fostering drew the attention of an even wider audience simply because most evacuees did go into foster homes or billets. In the first evacuation, the children were often placed in a haphazard manner: Jewish children were put with non-Jewish; Catholics with Scottish Protestants; young children with very old foster parents. Most reception authorities eventually appointed full-time visitors to inspect the foster homes and gradually a body of expertise in fostering was accumulated. Thus in Oxford the Barnet House Study Group and Boyd in Scotland noted that foster children settled most happily with foster parents of the same social class. The large scale study of evacuees in Cambridge led Issacs and her colleagues to conclude that foster children did best in homes where there were other children (whether their own siblings or the foster parents' children); where the foster parents were in their thirties or forties; and where there was regular contact with their own parents. She added that 'The nervous, anxious child is more happily placed in a quiet, conventional home where, if he is not actually alone, he at least has an opportunity to keep to himself and follow his own interests. The over-active, aggressive child is happier in a tolerant, free and easy home with companions of his own age, where he has not to fall back too much on his own resources.'

Of course, the Poor Law and voluntary societies had fostered children before the war. But the scale of fostering under the evacuation stimulated interest and research. It was acknowledged that fostering was a desirable way of looking after other people's children, that the population did contain many couples capable of undertaking the task, and that it was a process which required skilled staff to match children with substitute parents and to supervise the placements. In a broadcast at the end of war, Donald Winnicott said, 'One certain value to be got out of evacuation (itself a tragic thing) is that all of you who have succeeded in keeping an evacuee have come to understand the difficulties, as well as the rewards, that belong to caring for other people's children.'

So evacuation led to greater study of the methods of caring for separated children. It also watered the seeds of the idea of prevention, that the best practice would be to avoid children having to be separated from their parents at all. Burlingham and Freud commended the residential nurseries for the care they gave to children but they also had to note that full-time institutional care for young children did impair their emotional development and was not a complete substitute for the personal care of their parents. Lucy Faithfull, on returning to Islington after the war, participated in an investigation of children who had not been evacuated and who had stayed with their parents. She found that, compared with the evacuees, 'they were taller, despite missing school meals, were heavier and were emotionally better balanced. The evacuees scored higher on education.' She continued, 'that experience affected my subsequent work because I realized that wherever possible children should remain with their parents.'

It must be added that, during the war, parents did strive to be with their children. Jean Heywood argued that evacuation, far from weakening the family, actually demonstrated its strengths for 'In spite of carefully contrived plans to evacuate mothers and young children and school children to safe areas, they refused to remain divided and gradually, in ones and threes and then in groups and crowds, they returned to their homes and family circle, preferring to stay together under danger than to be separated and safe.' If the family unit was both central to society and beneficial to all, then a few social workers like Lucy Faithfull began to conclude that in the future welfare agencies could not rest content with maximizing the quality of methods of care for separated children but would have to ask for the powers and resources to help vulnerable families to stay together.

Social workers

The importance of caring for separated children thus came to the fore in the war years. But who would do the caring? Who would develop and oversee the improving methods of care? The answer had to be the welfare officers (or social workers as they were increasingly called). One of the significant side effects of the evacuation was the growth, even the establishment, of the occupation of social work.

The need for full-time welfare officers was most quickly perceived in the reception areas. Foster homes for the evacuees not only had to be found, they also had to be inspected and supported. Simultaneously, evacuated mothers with small children often met problems concerning finances, accommodation, health and worries about their husbands. These difficulties required a more personal touch than could be supplied by clerical staff. The case for welfare workers was clear, but who would pay? The Ministry of Health agreed on financial support but only for duties specifically relating to evacuees. Thereafter, the reception authorities did increase their numbers of welfare staff. In some cases, they shared the funding and appointed welfare officers who also undertook some of the usual welfare duties of their education departments.

The reception areas and other authorities were also faced with an increasing number of unmarried mothers wanting support and advice on where to obtain a maternity bed, what finances were available, how to find accommodation and whether or not the baby should be adopted. In 1943, the Ministry of Health issued a circular which recommended that local authorities appoint social workers for these duties. The circular marked an end to Poor Law responsibility for unmarried mothers and placed them fully within the scope of local health departments. Accordingly, health departments appointed eighty-one new social workers while some subsidised the moral welfare work of church voluntary societies.

The expansion must not be exaggerated for some authorities failed to respond. However, the new social work trend was clear.

The end of the war could have seen the decline of the new appointments. There were a number of reasons why it did not. Even in 1946, some 38,000 evacuees, mainly mothers with young children, had no homes to which to return. They remained in digs, hostels and requisitioned houses where welfare workers attempted to help them. In addition, the new welfare and social workers had established their worth. The growth of staff in nurseries and hostels had also added to the whole welfare sector. The hostels' links with psychiatric social workers, child guidance teams and psychiatrists also added to the respectability of some sections of the new social work. And at Government level, the war had led the Ministry of Health to appoint its first chief welfare officer to oversee the twenty-eight regional officers. Social work had become a small growth industry and, with a Welfare State in prospect, was likely to become even larger.

The impression must not be given that social work expertise was developed only in the reception areas. Bombed-out families also required immediate practical and emotional support and some authorities in the danger zones began to employ workers specifically for this task. The need for such social work skills became even more evident when evacuees returned, particularly at the end of the war. Even children who were longing to be home faced difficulties of adapting to parents whom they might have seen but rarely for a considerable length of time. And a few children did return reluctantly. In *No Time To Wave Goodbye* Ben Wicks tells of one girl, evacuated from a poor area of Hammersmith, who went to a colonel's home where she got used to comfort, being driven to school and servants. The war ended and she wrote, 'Then my lovely world crumbled.' No doubt such extreme changes of conditions were rare but, as Titmuss wrote in *Problems of Social Policy*:

*Circumstances in which guilt, conflict and anxiety could
flourish during the phase of reunion are easy to visualise.
There was the child, perhaps a little neglected emotionally,*

perhaps, in consequence, a little wayward, returning from a long stay in an evacuation hostel to a home where it was suddenly petted, spoilt and smothered with affection. There was the father, still a stranger to his child, back from from the Army with romantic, sentimentalised ideas about domesticity and parenthood. There was the mother, wanting, perhaps, not an independent, self-willed little girl but a small and helpless baby again. And there was the child, accustomed for what had seemed an eternity ... to a quiet and spacious middle-class home returning to a crowded, noisy home in a slum.

The re-formulation of some families did provoke a number of personal difficulties which, some local authorities perceived, required the listening ear and the skilled counselling of social workers.

The expansion of social work numbers also occurred in the voluntary sector where agencies had increased their involvement with evacuees and unmarried mothers. The national child care societies and bodies like the National Council for the Unmarried Mother and her Child were already well established. In addition, the bombs and the evacuation also sparked off at least one new and eventually very influential voluntary body, The Family Service Units. They started as pacifists who determined to help the most poverty-stricken and homeless in the midst of the bombing. In Liverpool, a number constituted themselves as a branch of the Pacifist Service Unit in 1940 and took in homeless families. Before long, it was in charge of five emergency rest centres. When the bombing lulled, they continued to help the families, organizing camps and holidays and relating with those outside the reach of other agencies. Other Pacifist Service Units did similar work and later they changed the name to the Family Service Units. Many, not all, of the workers and volunteers were motivated by a Christianity which looked to the medium of friendship as a means of serving their neighbour. Living amongst the most deprived and often rejected members of society, they pioneered a form of social work which was more informal but no less committed as that in the larger agencies.

Central government, local authorities and voluntary agencies thus all contributed to the emergence of the social work occupation. A constant theme amongst its practitioners was that social work was more than common sense and required people trained in certain skills. These skills included knowledge of the law and welfare procedure, understanding of human growth and development, and insights into the needs of deprived children, single parents and other groupings. This period also saw the attempt by social workers to identify a common thread between different kinds of social work, between those who dealt with children, the elderly, the physically handicapped or the mentally ill. This thread was called social casework which was regarded as the basic skill of social work. Clare Britton declared, 'It was during the war that social casework won final recognition.' She explained that the evacuation threw up such personal needs that voluntary helpers and unqualified staff could not cope. Trained social workers, including psychiatric social workers, had to be called in because they were equipped to help the most troubled by the application of casework. In her chapter 'Child care' in C. Morris' *Social Case-Work* Britton went on to define casework as:

the process of giving such attention and study to an individual and his environment as will enable him and the caseworker to work together, using all the resources available in the whole situation, to supply some need which is more than he could deal with by himself.

The Children's Committees

In 1943, the Ministry of Health began planning the return of the evacuees. The internal committee set up for this purpose identified the problem of what to do with those evacuee children who would have no homes to return to because their parents had been killed or had gone missing. (Its estimate of 10,000 children in this plight proved too high but they had pinpointed a real need and many evacuee children were still in the reception areas in 1948).

The committee's worries about these children contributed to concerns about other children, not evacuees, whose parents had been killed at home or abroad. In addition, the war was seen as unsettling family life in three other ways. First, a rise in delinquency figures was attributed to the absence of fathers in the Forces and the frequent closure of schools due to bombing. Whatever the reasons, the statistics were that the number of boys under fourteen years found guilty of indictable offences rose from 14,724 in 1938 to 22,525 in 1944: figures for girls were 835 to 1,558. Amongst those aged 14–17, the rise was from 11,645 to 14,620 for males and 912 to 1,846 for females. Second, the increase in the number of children found by courts to be in need of care and protection or beyond control—from 879 in 1939 to 1,908 in 1944—was also attributed to the unsettling effects of war on family life. Third, the sharp rise in illegitimate births, from 25,942 (4.19 per cent of all live births) in 1939 to 64,064 (9.35 per cent) in 1945, was also seen as stemming from war conditions. John Costello in *Love, Sex and War 1939–45* states:

So many fathers were absent from home in military service that war-time adolescents were deprived of parental supervision and discipline at a critical stage in their emotional and sexual development. Girls could leave school at fourteen, and there were plenty of servicemen to provide excitement as an escape from war time deprivations.

Even if illegitimacy rates were to decrease after the war, it was argued that public bodies might have to be responsible for many born during the war.

These factors indicated a growing number of needy children. But which Government and local government bodies should look after them? The committee within the Ministry of Health reflected the public mood when it stated that the children should not be left with bodies associated with the Poor Law. Instead, in 1944, it came up with the suggestion that a new Children's Committee should be established in every county and county borough, to be responsible not just for abandoned evacuee children but for all children separated from their parents.

The possibility of a new local committee provoked some early rivalry at central government level as to which Ministry would have overall control—officials at the Ministry of Health and the Board of Education expressed an interest. One view put forward was that deprived children should be administratively kept apart from the stigma of being associated with delinquent children. Others rejoined that the problems of both stemmed from family malfunctioning. In 1943, a Conservative Party committee, chaired by R.A. Butler, published a report, *Youth Astray*, recommending that old ideas about punishing delinquents be replaced by an emphasis on 'education as a means of reform.' Some saw this as ammunition for the case that the Board of Education (soon to be the Ministry of Education) should have both deprived and delinquent youngsters put under its wing. But no matter what the mix of children or which Ministry won command, the important fact was that war and the evacuation had given rise, at Government level, for proposals for a new local committee to specialize in children separated from their parents.

Lady Allen again

By 1944, the evacuation had contributed to improvements in the methods of child care, to the emergence of the occupation of social work, to the anticipation of an increase in the numbers of needy children, and to proposals for a new local authority Children's Committee. All that was needed to persuade Parliament to draw these strands together into a new children's service was a public campaign. The stage was set for the ubiquitous Lady Allen.

Marjory Allen was in the midst of her lobbying for better day care when, as she wrote, 'My own efforts during the war to extend an understanding of nursery education led me, by chance, to stumble on another subject which kept me occupied for several years.' While visiting a school, she noticed a group of children who seemed listless and unhappy. On learning that they were from a children's home, she determined to investigate the plight of deprived children. Later, while at a seaside town, she learned that 'there was an evacuated Home nearby, but that local people who wanted to be friendly to the children had been discouraged from asking them out.' Lady Allen was not the type to be discouraged and gained entrance to the home run by a religious order. She was horrified at the lack of toys, the absence of personal care and the isolation from the community. She recorded that she 'mentioned bed-wetting, the subject that was always cropping up among people caring for disturbed evacuated children' and discovered that persistent offenders were punished by caning. Thereafter, Lady Allen visited a number of voluntary (or charitable) and local authority homes. She acknowledged that some, especially the new hostels, were examples of good practice but she considered that most were inadequate and resulted in stunted lives for the children. She then wrote her famous letter to *The Times* which was published on 15 July 1944 and read as follows:

Sir, Thoughtful consideration is being given to many fundamental problems, but in reconstruction plans one section of the community has, so far, been entirely forgotten.

I write of those children who, because of their family misfortune, find themselves under the guardianship of a Government department or one of the many charitable organizations. The public are, for the most part, unaware that many thousands of these children are being brought up under repressive conditions that are generations out of date and are unworthy of our traditional care for children. Many who are orphaned, destitute, or neglected still live under the chilly stigma of 'charity'; too often they form groups isolated from the main stream of life and education, and few of them know the comfort and security of individual affection. A letter does not allow space for detailed evidence.

In many 'Homes', both charitable and public, the willing staff are, for the most part, overworked, underpaid, and untrained; indeed there is no recognized system of training. Inspection, for which the Ministry of Health, the Home Office, or the Board of Education may be nominally responsible, is totally inadequate, and few standards are established or expected. Because no one Government department is fully responsible, the problem is the more difficult to tackle.

179

A public inquiry, with full Government support, is urgently needed to explore this largely uncivilised territory. Its mandate should be to ascertain whether the public and charitable organizations are, in fact, enabling these children to lead full and happy lives and to make recommendations how the community can compensate them for the family life they have lost. In particular, the inquiry should investigate what arrangements can be made (by regional reception centres or in other ways) for the careful consideration of the individual children before they are finally placed with foster-parents or otherwise provided for; how the use of large residential homes can be avoided; how staff can be appropriately trained and ensured adequate salaries and suitable conditions of work, and how central administrative responsibility can be set and can be maintained by adequate inspection.

The social upheaval caused by the war has not only increased this army of unhappy children, but presents the opportunity for transforming their conditions. The Education Bill and the White Paper on the Health Services have alike ignored the problem and the opportunity.

Yours sincerely,
Marjory Allen of Hurtwood.

The response to the letter was astonishing. *The Times* received more letters about child care than on any other subject including the war. And this at a time when Britain was being subjected to the doodle-bugs. Letters of support came from people as varied as Susan Issacs, Nancy Astor and Bernard Shaw along with those from former residents of children's homes. After sixty published letters and two 'round-ups', *The Times* had to bring the correspondence to a close. One reason for the enormous public interest was that evacuation had already made the issue of child care of general interest. Commenting on debates in Parliament, Roy Parker noted, 'some MPs referred quite explicitly to their interest in the problems of children deprived of a normal home life having been aroused by their contact with evacuees.'

The Government had to take some action and on 7 December 1944 the Home Secretary, Herbert Morrison, announced that he intended to set up a committee 'to inquire into existing methods of providing for children deprived of a normal home life.' However, he did not announce the membership of the committee and seemed in no hurry to do so despite pressure exerted by Lady Allen and her supporters both inside and outside of Parliament. The matter came tragically to a head when, on 9 January 1945, a child died in his foster home.

Dennis, Terence and Freddy O'Neill had been committed to the care of Newport County Borough Council on the grounds of parental neglect. Their older brother, Tom, was sent to an approved school. Foster homes in the Borough were hard to find because of the influx of evacuees and the Newport Education Department had to go as far as Herefordshire whose Education Department agreed to supervise the children. The foster home broke down and Newport's school attendance officer travelled over and found a replacement home for Terence and Freddy in Shropshire. The officer drove around with the thirteen-year-old Dennis, again finding homes full of evacuees. Eventually, a Mr and Mrs Gough took Dennis into their isolated farm (where he was later joined by Terence). The boys were subjected to a life of terror with insufficient food and regular beatings from Mr Gough. Under-fed, bruised and battered, Dennis died.

The death and subsequent prosecutions of the Goughs became a national scandal and the Government had to respond. On 8 March 1945, Herbert Morrison named the members of two committees of inquiry, one for England and Wales chaired by Myra Curtis and one for Scotland chaired by James Clyde. Further, Sir James Monckton was appointed to examine the O'Neill tragedy.

Monckton acted quickly and his report was published in May. He attributed blame to the inadequate supervision by Newport Council and, to a lesser extent, by Shropshire. Their deficiencies he related to a lack of communication between various departments. Marjory Allen—to the surprise of some omitted from the Curtis Committee—seized upon the Monckton report to reinforce her campaign. She made the case for one council committee (and its one department) to be devoted just to deprived children and to be run by qualified staff.

Curtis and Clyde

The Curtis and Clyde Committees reported in 1946. They had received the views of the leaders of statutory and voluntary welfare agencies, they had visited many children's homes, and they listened to expert witnesses including Lady Allen, Susan Issacs, Geraldine Aves, Clare Britton and Donald Winnicott. The Clyde Committee, in Scotland, reported first and argued strongly for a new emphasis on fostering because 'By this means the child should get the nearest approximation to family life.' After fostering, it recommended small children's homes run by trained staff. It criticized the fact that, in Scotland, five statutory bodies were in charge of 17,607 children while voluntary agencies looked after another 4,788. It continued that it was 'inappropriate to leave these children in the hands of a Public Assistance Authority with a Poor Law outlook' and proposed, instead, the creation of a new committee charged exclusively with the welfare of deprived children.

The Curtis Report, four times as long as its Scottish counterpart, enumerated 124,000 children within its scope. These included 5,200 former evacuees who had been unable to return to their homes after the war. The Committee had made a detailed investigation of residential establishments, including some old workhouses which still contained children. While visiting some excellent homes, it concluded that far too many were too large, too isolated, too institutionalized. It argued that deprived children fared far better in foster homes.

The masterly analysis of the Curtis Report ends with sixty-two recommendations of which the following were particularly important:

The preferred order of caring for children unable to live with their parents, relatives or guardians was first adoption (although this was applicable to only a few), then fostering and finally residential care.

The public care of such children should be the responsibility of just one local authority committee, to be called the Children's Committee, with its own Department and to be overseen by one central government Ministry.

The Children's Committee should employ its own executive officer, 'an officer of high standing and qualifications' (later called the Children's Officer).

Training should be introduced for all staff.

The Curtis and Clyde Reports are milestones in the British history of children separated from their parents. No previous reports had so clearly identified the failings of the current systems: no previous reports had concentrated solely on their well-being: no previous reports had made such an unanswerable case for a local authority committee concerned only with them: no previous reports had so strongly insisted on the necessity for training for child care staff. Perhaps the spirit of the reports is summed up in a part of the Curtis Report which explains that the core of the new work would be 'establishing and maintaining a continuing personal relation between the child deprived of a home and the official of the local authority responsible for looking after him.' Clearly the Committee envisaged committed and long-serving staff who would be 'the friend of those particular children through their childhood and adolescence up to the age of sixteen or eighteen.'

The Children Act 1948

All political parties accepted the recommendations of the Reports and the Children Bill proceeded smoothly through Parliament and, as the Children Act, became law on 5 July1948. It stipulated that local authorities be given a duty to receive into their care children under the age of seventeen whose parents or guardians were unable to provide for them and whose welfare required the intervention of the local authority. It established Children's Committees which were also to take over responsibility for children committed to local authorities by the courts, for protecting private foster children, for supervising certain adoption placements and for inspecting voluntary homes. The Home Office was later designated as the responsible central government Ministry.

The Act decreed that local authorities had a duty to board-out (foster) children in their care and, when this was 'not practicable or desirable for the time being' to maintain them in residential homes. The Act gave some recognition to the child's natural family by stipulating that the local authority should, if in the interests of the welfare of the child, endeavour to secure that the care of a child who came into care was taken over by parents, guardians or relatives. However, it did not give local authorities clear powers to undertake preventative work to avoid children having to come into public care. This proved an unfortunate omission and, in the 1950s, Lucy Faithfull and her colleagues had to campaign for such powers. But the future Lady Faithfull would have been delighted with one other provision of the Act, namely its decree to establish an Advisory Council on Child Care to advise the Secretary of State on the promotion of training.

If the Curtis and Clyde Reports were stepping stones, the Children Act was a landmark in legislation for deprived children as can be seen by comparing its provisions with the situation in 1939. At that time the care of children was fragmented amongst a number of departments whose main interests were in other spheres, such as education or health: but 1948 saw the creation of a single, new department just for deprived children. In 1939 some children were still under the auspices of the Poor Law legislation: 1948 witnessed the remaining children removed from the Public Assistance Departments and, indeed, the Act became law on the same day as the National Assistance Act buried the Poor Law for good. In 1939 the majority of children in public or voluntary care were in institutions: 1948 saw legislation which made it a duty to pursue fostering. In 1939 training for child care workers was in its infancy: from 1948 it multiplied. In 1939 services for children operated within a social framework of limited welfare provision for poor families: by 1948 poverty had not been removed but the Welfare State had established numerous benefits which enabled more families to cope with their own children.

The Children Act 1948 expressed an enormous social jump forward. It did not happen suddenly and certainly cannot be attributed just to Lady Allen and her famous letter. The need for and the case for reform had been whispered throughout the earlier part of the century. It was evolution not revolution. Yet when the whisper grew into a shout during the 1940s, the changes came so rapidly that it appeared like a revolution. The evacuation contributed to that speed of change in three main ways.

First, it propelled the needs of children into the public and political arena. As Roy Parker explained in his chapter 'The gestation of reform: the Children Act 1948' in Bean and MacPherson's *Approaches to Welfare*, elderly and handicapped persons also had needs and wants yet there was no Old Persons Act, no committee established just for the handicapped, no departments for them alone. The reason was that evacuation had pushed the needs of children forward just at the time when welfare legislation started rolling.

Second, evacuation popularized the method of fostering. When, on 5 July, the new Children's Committees took over they found that most children, who had been looked after by the Education, Public Assistance and Health departments, were in institutions. The exception was among the remainder of the evacuees, for two-thirds of them were in foster homes. Evacuation established fostering as the method for looking after children living apart from their parents.

Third, evacuation demonstrated that separated children required the services of full-time trained welfare staff. Moreover, it led to an expansion of the number of social workers so that more were available to be recruited by the new Children's Departments.

Good from evil

Wars, disaster, pain, death, trouble the hearts and minds of both theologians and the 'man and woman in the street'. Why does God allow suffering? The missionary doctor, Paul Brand, has experienced his share of personal pain and witnessed communities in pain abroad. In his book, with Philip Yancey, *Pain: The Gift Nobody Wants* he reflects deeply and concludes that national disasters are not God's way of punishing human beings—if they were then God, as in the Bible, would make clear who is being punished and why. Suffering and pain cannot be satisfactorily explained yet, oddly, they can give rise to good. Brand has been impressed in India by the way in which a whole community responds to disasters and so improves respect and care for each other.

The Second World War, the Blitz, the V1s and the V2s, the evacuation, meant injury, destruction, death, separation, physical and emotional pain. Warfare. Yet it did engender responses which were noble, sacrificial, good. Interestingly, Dr Brand was in Britain 'during the Blitz, when an entire city rallied around the common purpose of helping people who were in pain. A volunteer corps of nurses' aides sprang up spontaneously. People started checking regularly on their neighbours. The injured were not hidden away, but rather honoured.' Further, the responses to evacuation contributed strongly to the pressures which led to the Children Act 1948 and the new Children's Departments. From warfare to child care. Father Groser insisted that God did not bring about war but did allow humankind the decision making powers which it exercised to choose war. However, he continued, the Christian message is that God does work in the hearts of men and women to bring forth good even from the depths of evil.

This makes sense to me. Now, in the mid-1990s, I work in the vast Easterhouse estate in Glasgow where high unemployment and poverty is tolerated by a Government which has scorned the Welfare State of the 1940s. I regard the readiness to allow intense social deprivations in the midst of an affluent society as evil. It is an evil which drives some into the further evils of drugs and crime. Yet I see others who respond to oppose evil. Local residents band together to form a food co-op so as to provide cheaper food for the community. Other low-income citizens initiate a credit union to make low interest loans to neighbours who otherwise are drawn into the snares of the loan sharks with their high interest rates and violence as a means of enforcement. There is the lion-hearted Salvation Army officer who, when Government legislation virtually abolished grants for new items for people dependent upon Income Support, started a huge store—God's Warehouse—to provide cheap albeit second-hand cookers, fires and tables. There are the Sisters of Charity combining the spiritual and social in a way that gives both personal comfort and collective strength. The lesson learnt in the war is repeated today. Evil cannot be justified, but human beings can respond to bring positives out of the negatives.

From evacuation to child care

And some of those people caught up in the evil of war and the distress of evacuation were themselves later to be found in the very children's services which evolved from it. In *No Time To Wave Goodbye* Ben Wicks records an account by Freda Risley who, as an evacuee, felt rejected by her family. Later she wrote,

> *On the positive side, since I work with children, I've learned four invaluable lessons. I never take an adult's word against a child's at face value; I respect what kids have to say. I credit them with more understanding and awareness than is general. I know why battered kids never tell, and I'm pretty good at spotting when something is wrong.*

Eric and Anne Buchanan became Salvation Army officers at the hard end. Laurie Laken had a career in approved schools and children's homes before turning to youth work in the East End of London. John Vaizey, both hospitalized and evacuated, later established himself as a social scientist and wrote in *Scenes from Institutional Life,*

> *In the field of the social services, which is my own field, the trend is away from institutional care for deprived children. This is all to the good, and one longs for the day when the last children's home is burnt to the ground.*

Vaizey taught at the London School of Economics where his paths would have crossed with those of Dr Donald Winnicott and Clare Britton as they trained social work students preparing to join the Children's Departments. Lucy Faithfull, after the war, joined the new child care Inspectorate at the Home Office and later became the distinguished Children's Officer for Oxford. Today, in the House of Lords, she is known as 'the children's champion'.

As for me, with less distinction, I too worked as a child care officer for a Children's Department and then participated in the training of social workers before spending the next eighteen years working with children and families on projects located in two council estates. I don't know whether my experiences as an evacuee gave me insights into the needs of separated children. I don't know whether it shaped my decision to enter the children's services. I do know that it made me value the love of my mother and father and to appreciate the sacrifices they made to keep our family together. And it is this appreciation of loving families which drives the likes of us to strive for a society which equips parents with the resources to care for their children. But, if this is not possible, let there be services, akin to the Children's Departments, in which priority is given to personal care and attention for separated children. For the evacuation taught us that that is what children need.

Bibliography

B. Abel-Smith & P.Townsend, *The Poor And The Poorest*, Bell, 1965.

P. Addison, *The Road To 1945*, Pimlico, 1975.

P. Addison, 'On to the new Jerusalem', *The Guardian*, May 20th, 1994.

M. Allen, *Memoirs Of An Uneducated Lady*, Thames & Hudson, 1975.

C. Attlee, *As It Happened*, Heinemann, 1954.

H. Bannister and H. Ravden, 'The problem child and his environment', *British Journal of Psychology, vol. XXIV*, January 1944.

Barnett House Study Group, *London Children In War-Time Oxford*, Barnett House, 1947.

J. Beveridge, *Beveridge And His Plan*, Hodder & Stoughton, 1954.

P. Brand & P. Yancey, *Pain: The Gift Nobody Wants*, Marshall Pickering, 1994.

W. Boyd (editor), *Evacuation In Scotland*, University of London Press, 1944.

C. Britton, 'Child care', in C. Morris (editor), *Social Case-Work*, Faber & Faber, 1954.

D. Burlingham & A. Freud, *Children In War-Time*, Methuen, 1940.

A. Calder, *The People's War, 1939–45*, Jonathan Cape, 1969.

A. Calder, *The Myth Of The Blitz*, Jonathan Cape, 1991.

J. Chaplin, 'See thon evacuees', *Scottish Memories*, October, 1993.

Commission of the Churches, *Evacuation And The Churches*, Student Christian Movement Press, 1941.

P. Connolly (editor), *Evacuees At Dartington, 1940–45*, Dartington Hall, 1990.

J. Costello, *Love, Sex And War, 1939–45*, Pan Books, 1985.

R. Crompton, *William And The Evacuees*, Pan Macmillan, 1987.

S. Ferguson & H. Fitzgerald, *Studies In The Social Services*, H.M.S.O. and Longmans, Green & Co., 1954.

J. Groser, *Politics And Persons*, Student Christian Movement Press, 1949.

J. Heywood, *Children In Care*, Routledge & Kegan Paul, 1959.

B. Holman, *Putting Families First*, Macmillan Education, 1988.

B. Holman, *Good Old George: The Life Of George Lansbury*, Lion Publishing, 1990.

B. Holman, *'Not Like Any Other Home', Herbert White And The Children's Home & Mission*, Campaign Books, 1994.

M. Hughes, *No Cake, No Jam: A War-Time Childhood*, Heinemann, 1994.

R. Inglis, *The Children's War*, Fontana, 1990.

S. Issacs (editor), *The Cambridge Evacuation Survey*, Methuen, 1941.

A. Jones, *Farewell Manchester*, Didsbury Press, 1989.

S. Lawrence, *The Children's Welfare In War Time*, Labour Party, 1940.

J. Macnicol, 'The effect of the evacuation of schoolchildren on official attitudes to state intervention', in H. Smith (editor), *British Society In The Second World War*, Manchester University Press, 1984.

L. Manning, *A Life For Education*, Gollancz, 1970.

A. Marwick, *The Home Front*, Thames & Hudson, 1976.

K. Morgan, *The People's Peace. British History 1945–1989*, Oxford University Press, 1990.

R. Parker, 'The gestation of reform: the Children Act 1948', in P. Bean & S. MacPherson (editors), *Approaches To Welfare*, Routledge & Kegan Paul, 1983.

B. Rodgers, *The Battle Against Poverty, vol. 2*, Routledge & Kegan Paul, 1969.

D. Sheridan (editor), *Wartime Women*, Heinemann, 1990.

E. Shinwell, *The Britain I Want*, MacDonald, 1943.

St Loe Strachey, *Borrowed Children*, John Murray, 1940.

J. Stroud, *13 Penny Stamps*, Hodder & Stoughton, 1971.

A.J.P. Taylor, *English History 1914–45*, Pelican, 1987.

W. Temple, *The Hope Of A New World*, Student Christian Movement Press, 1940.

L. Thomas, *This Time Next Week*, Pan Books, 1971.

R. Titmuss, *Problems Of Social Policy*, H.M.S.O. and Longmans, Green & Co.

C. Townsend & E. Townsend, *War Wives*, Grafton Books, 1989.

J. Vaizey, *Scenes From Institutional Life*, Faber & Faber, 1959.

M. Wainwright, *The Blitz Of Bath*, Kingston Press, 1981.

B. Wicks, *No Time To Wave Good-bye*, Bloomsbury Publishing, 1988.

D. Winnicott, *The Child And The Outside World*, Tavistock Publications, 1957.

Women's Group On Public Welfare, *Our Towns: A Close-Up*, Oxford University Press, 1943.

Index